Key Stage 3

Experimental and Investigative Skills

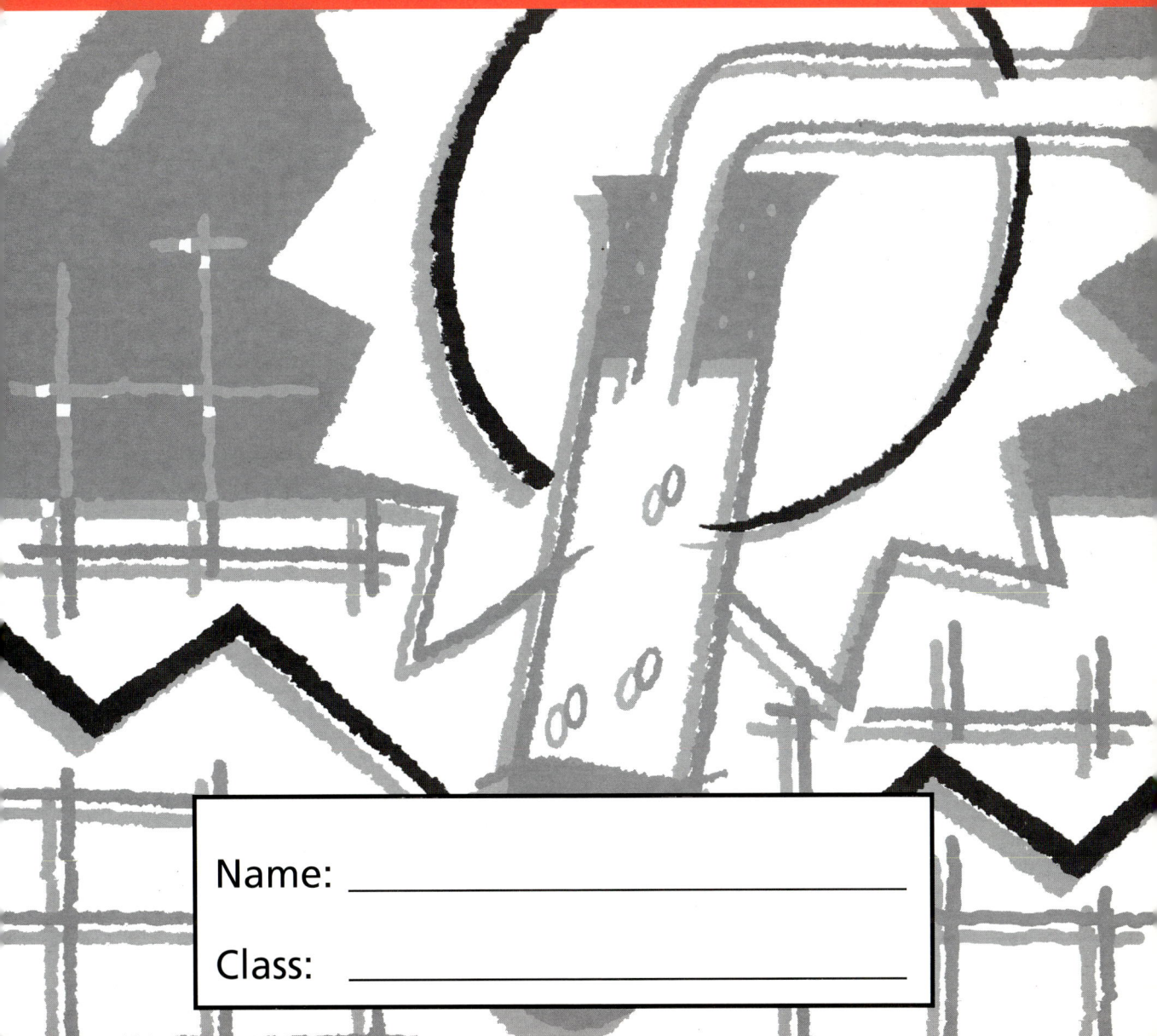

Name: _____

Class: _____

Science

Richard Barnett
Marilyn Brodie
Derek Green
Terry Hudson

Every effort has been made to trace copyright holders and to obtain their permission for the use of copyright material. The authors and publishers will gladly receive information enabling them to rectify any error or omission in subsequent editions.

First published 1999

Letts Educational
9–15 Aldine Street
London W12 8AW
Tel 0181 740 2270
Fax 0181 740 2280

Text: © Richard Barnett, Marilyn Brodie, Derek Green, Terry Hudson 1999

Design and illustrations © BPP (Letts Educational) Ltd 1999

Design and page layout: Ken Vail Graphic Design, Cambridge

Illustrations: Simon Girling & Associates (Mike Lacey),
            Ken Vail Graphic Design

British Library Cataloguing-in-Publication Data

A CIP record for this book is available from the British Library

ISBN 1 84085 221 6

Printed and Bound in Great Britain

Letts Educational is the trading name of
BPP (Letts Educational) Ltd

Contents

How to use this book   iv

Planning experimental work

1 Tips 1   2
2 Asking questions   4
3 Predicting   6
4 Trial runs   8
5 Fair testing 1   10
6 Fair testing 2   12
7 Range of results   14
8 Investigations in the field   16
9 Types of measurements   18
10 Measuring instruments   19

Obtaining evidence

11 Tips 2   21
12 Reading scales 1   22
13 Reading scales 2   24
14 Collecting enough results   26
15 Tables of results   29

Analysing evidence and drawing conclusions

16 Tips 3   31
17 Bar charts   32
18 Graphs 1   33
19 Graphs 2   34
20 Graphs 3   36
21 Graphs 4   38
22 Graphs 5   40
23 Describing results   42
24 Describing patterns in graphs   44
25 Writing conclusions   46
26 Types of data   49

Considering the strength of the data

27 Tips 4   51
28 Evaluating investigations   52

Investigation grid   56

How to use this book

At Key Stage 3 (Years 7 to 9) you will perform investigations in Science, building on the work you did at Key Stage 2. These scientific investigations will be in four main parts:

1 Planning experimental work
2 Obtaining evidence
3 Analysing evidence and drawing conclusions
4 Considering the strength of the data

To start with you will practise certain parts of an investigation or particular skills. Eventually you will be asked to perform a whole investigation from start to finish. **This book** is designed to help you practise each individual skill so that you can improve your work on science investigations.

Some activities are more demanding than others. At the bottom of each page you will see the National Curriculum levels covered by the activities on that page. The level you reach in investigative work forms an important part of your overall National Curriculum level in Science at the end of Year 9.

At the back of the book is a grid of levels. When you have practised the various skills you could try looking up the skill in the grid. It will give you a very good idea of how you are doing.

As you do an investigation or activity at school you could find and use the appropriate section in this book to help you. Check the grid to give an idea of the level you are working at.

The activities are organised into the sequence of stages you would work through when doing a whole investigation. Pick the activities from the book that will help you with the work you are doing at the time.

At the beginning of each of the four parts of the book, there is a **Tips** section. This is designed to give you helpful ideas that you can use to improve the next investigation you do. There is space for you to jot down important things that you find out as you work. Listen to advice from your teacher during and after each investigation and write down anything you want to remember. It is important that you get into the habit of returning to the Tips section as you learn new skills. In this way you can build up your own list of advice and suggestions for improvements.

Also included at the bottom of each page are the links to the Classbook (Letts Key Stage 3 Science). These links will guide you to some of the science knowledge that will be helpful during your investigative work.

Planning experimental work

This diagram shows the important ideas you will cover in this section.

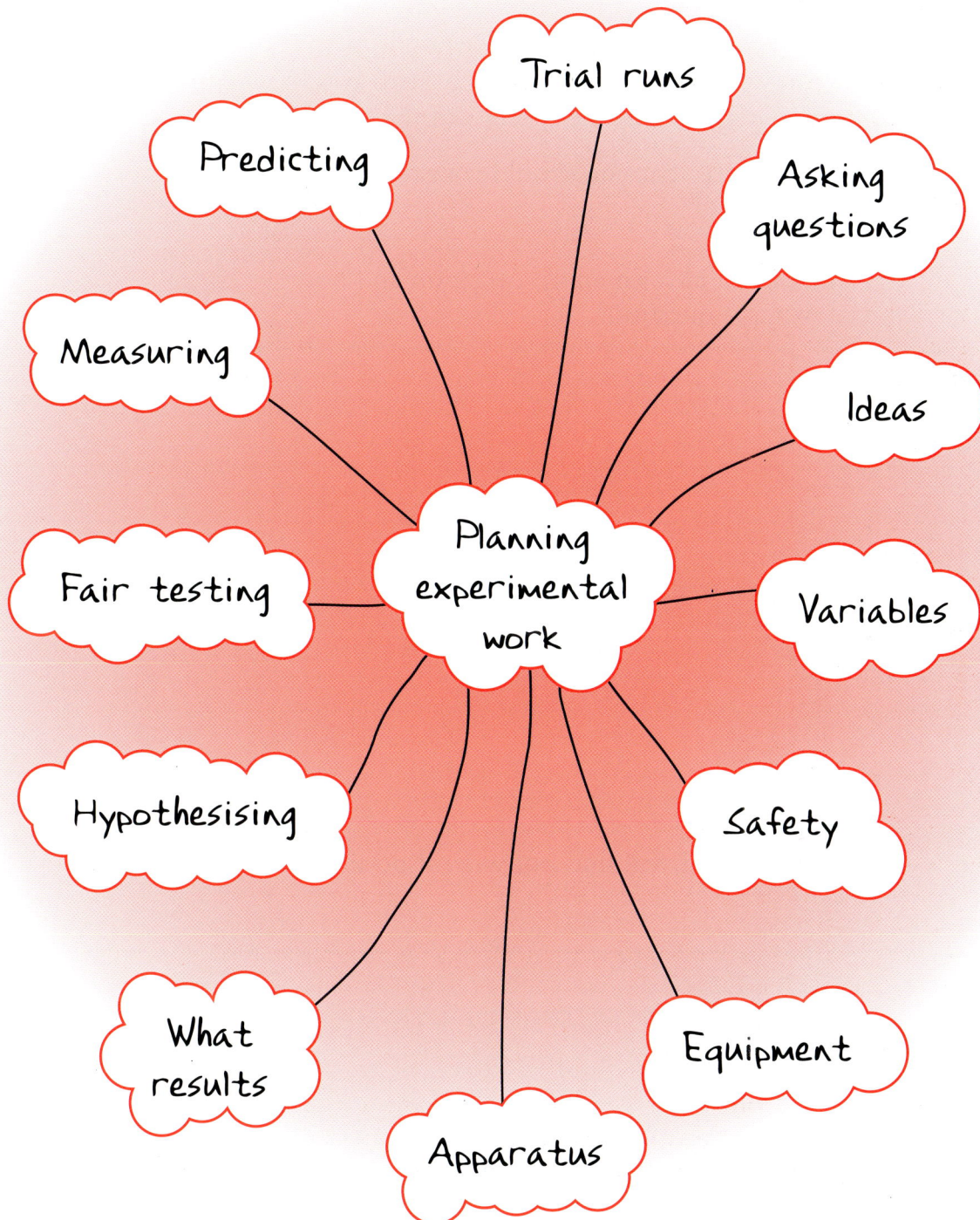

Trial runs

Predicting

Asking questions

Measuring

Ideas

Planning experimental work

Fair testing

Variables

Hypothesising

Safety

What results

Equipment

Apparatus

Improving my ability to plan experimental work

When you work through the first part of the book you will pick up tips and advice on planning. Your teacher or other pupils in your group may help you. When you find out something which helps you to **improve your planning**, write it down in the spaces below.

There are **eight** main areas that you should cover when you are planning. These are:

1 How do I think of an idea for an investigation and how do I write this down as a question?

....

....

....

2 Do I need to make a trial run of my investigation?

....

....

....

3 How do I predict what I will find out when I do my investigation?

....

....

....

4 What is the difference between the variable I am investigating and the variables that I need to control?

5 How many observations or measurements do I need to make and over what range?

6 What do I do when I am involved in fieldwork and cannot control all the variables?

7 How do I select apparatus and equipment?

8 What must I remember about using equipment safely?

When you start an investigation you will need to decide what you want to investigate. You will start by asking a **question**. You will then suggest what you think you might find out (a **prediction**).

A scientific question should have two parts:

- a question you can test
- a prediction.

Example

Dafydd had been doing some work in science on how animals keep warm. He knew he could put some warm water in a beaker and see how quickly it cooled. He made a list of possible questions.

These were his questions:

Note that all Dafydd's questions have a question mark at the end and start with words like 'Do', 'Does', 'Which' and 'What'.

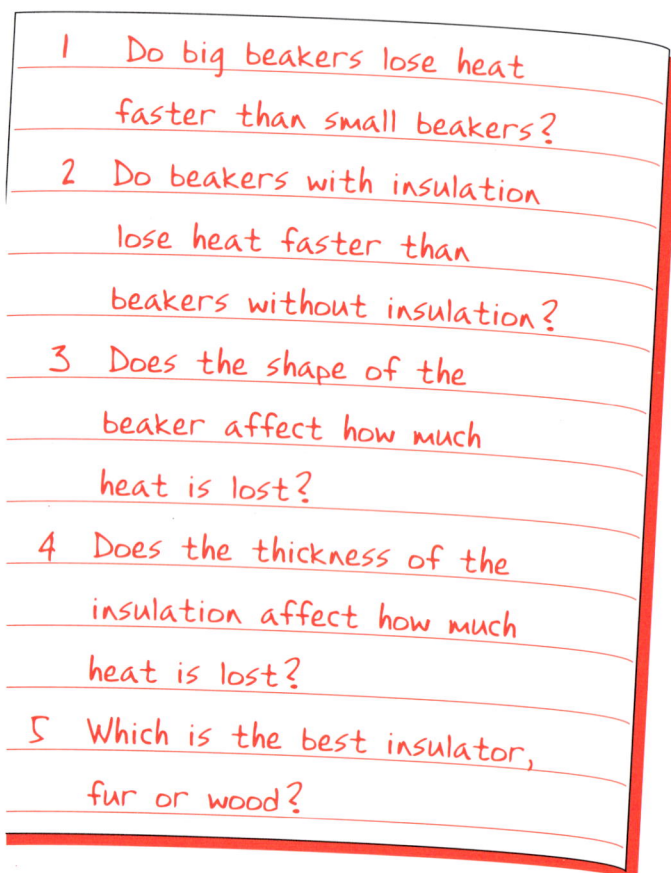

1 Do big beakers lose heat faster than small beakers?

2 Do beakers with insulation lose heat faster than beakers without insulation?

3 Does the shape of the beaker affect how much heat is lost?

4 Does the thickness of the insulation affect how much heat is lost?

5 Which is the best insulator, fur or wood?

National Curriculum links
- Experimental and investigative work
- Planning experimental work

To be working at levels 3–8 you will need to suggest ideas for investigations and make predictions.

Links with the Classbook

Unit 50
page 106

Now it's your turn

If you add sugar to water it eventually dissolves.

1 Discuss with your partner or group the following things:

   a What might you vary to see if you could get the sugar to dissolve more quickly?

   b Choose **three** of these variables.

2 For each variable write down a question in the spaces below. Remember two things:

   a all your questions should finish with a question mark

   b all your questions should start with words like, 'Do', 'Does', 'Which' or 'What'.

National Curriculum links
- Experimental and investigative work
- Planning experimental work

To be working at levels 3–8 you will need to suggest ideas for investigations and make predictions.

Links with the Classbook

Unit 52
pages 110–111

When you have decided what you want to investigate, you must try to say what you think will happen when you change your variable.

When you do this you will be **predicting**. There are two parts to a prediction:

- **What** results you think you'll find.

- A **reason** that explains why you think you will obtain these results. This reason should contain a **scientific** explanation. This can be based on something you have learned in science or from your own experience.

Scientists call this process 'making a **hypothesis**'.

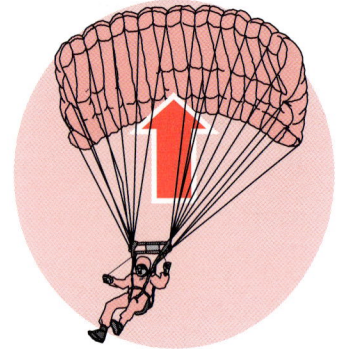

small canopy

Example

Jasmine had decided to perform an investigation with parachutes. She decided to vary the area of the parachute's canopy.

Her question was:
Do parachutes with large canopies fall more slowly than parachutes with smaller canopies?

This is what she thought she would find out:
The larger the area, the more slowly it will fall because...

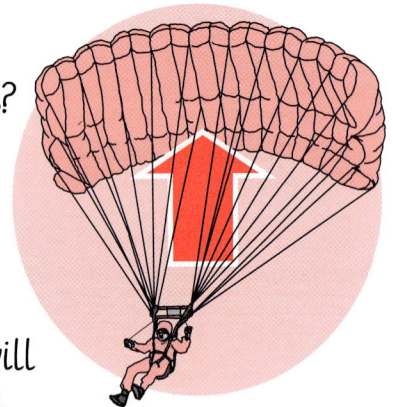

large canopy

Her scientific reason for this was:
...as the parachute falls, the larger canopy will catch more air creating more air resistance. This gives a greater upward force, therefore slowing down the parachute.

1 What are scientists doing when they hypothesise? ....

National Curriculum links
- Experimental and investigative work
- Planning experimental work

To be working at levels 3–8 you will need to suggest ideas for investigations, and make predictions.

Links with the Classbook

Unit 80
pages 170–171

Now it's your turn

2 For each of the questions below decide what you think you would find out and what your scientific reason would be.

a Does granulated sugar dissolve faster than cube sugar?

Prediction

....

....

Scientific reason

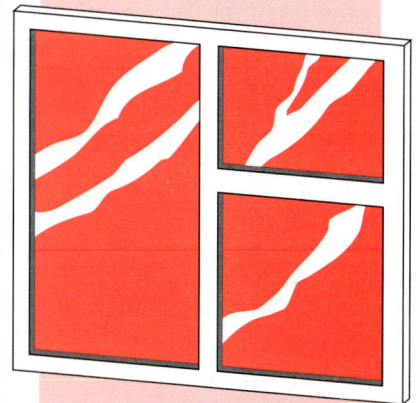

....

....

....

....

b Which is better at keeping heat in, single or double-glazing?

Prediction

....

....

Scientific reason

....

....

National Curriculum links
- Experimental and investigative work
- Planning experimental work

To be working at levels 3–8 you will need to suggest ideas for investigations and make predictions.

Links with the Classbook

Unit 52
pages 110–111

Unit 50
pages 106–107

Sometimes when you are planning an investigation there will be factors that are difficult to take into account without doing some 'trial runs'. This will usually involve:

- Trying out a particular piece of apparatus or measuring instrument so that you are familiar with it before the start of the investigation.

- Doing part of the investigation to see how long it takes before you plan the whole investigation.

- Deciding who is going to do what and trying out your jobs so that you can work as a team.

Example

Bijal and Gillian decided to investigate the question:

- Does the temperature of the water affect how quickly copper sulphate dissolves?

As a trial run they put 5g of copper sulphate powder into $500\,cm^3$ of water at 80°C. They stirred the solution for 10 seconds. They found that the copper sulphate dissolved very quickly so it was difficult to time how long it took. They decided to repeat their trial run using small copper sulphate crystals instead of powder, so the dissolving took longer and was easier to time.

Bijal and Gillian used the small crystals but still found that the copper sulphate dissolved very quickly.

1 Suggest **three** other things they could change to slow the dissolving down, while still being able to try a range of temperatures. Write your suggestions in the space below.

....

....

National Curriculum links
- Experimental and investigative work
- Planning experimental work

To be working at levels 4–6 you need to select suitable equipment and use it with care and precision, making enough observations and measurements for the task you are doing.

Links with the Classbook

Unit 52
pages 110–111

Now it's your turn

Now you are going to think about a trial run.
This time the topic is about cars running
down a ramp. You are investigating
the question:

■ How does the height of one end of a
ramp affect how fast a car runs down it?

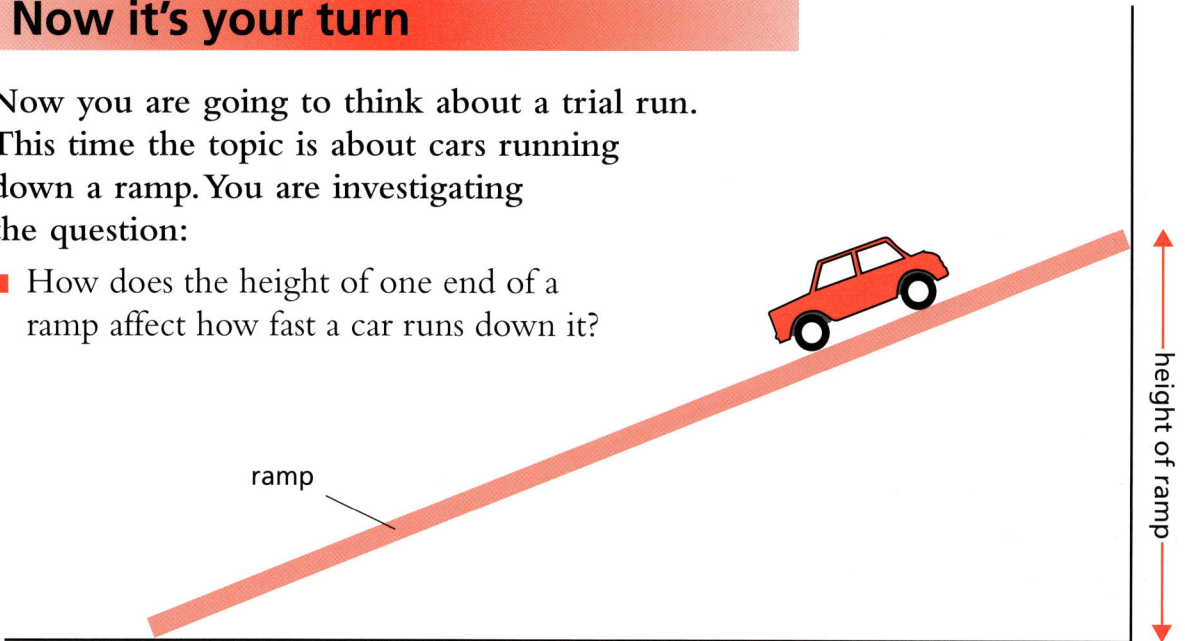

ramp

height of ramp

2 List the equipment you would need to use.

....

....

....

3 What trial runs would you choose to make and why?

....

....

....

National Curriculum links

■ Experimental and investigative work
■ Planning experimental work

*To be working at levels 4–6 you need to select suitable equipment
and use it with care and precision, making enough observations
and measurements for the task you are doing.*

**Links with the
Classbook**

**Units 77, 78
and 79**
pages 164–169

When you first start to do investigations you need to keep things simple. Start off by doing your investigation in two parts so that you can compare one part with the other.

Example

Helen is asking the question:

■ Does the temperature of the water affect how quickly sugar dissolves?

She set up two experiments:

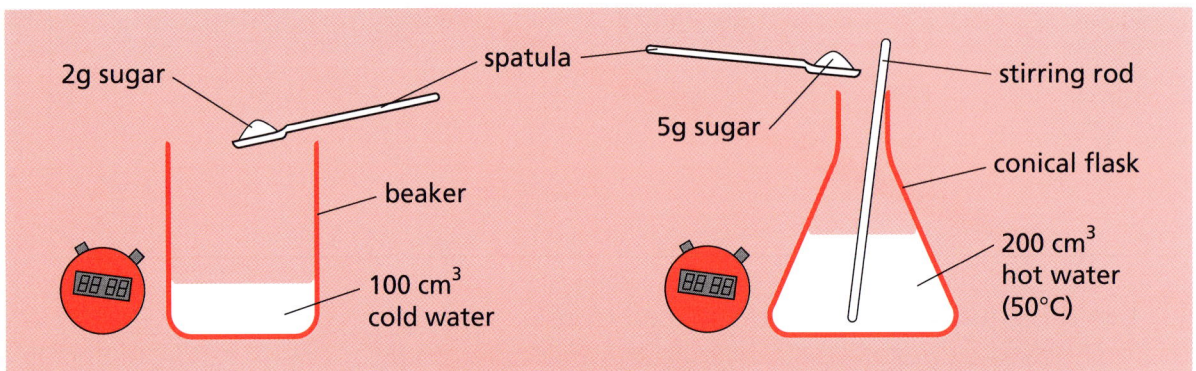

She added the sugar to the cold water and timed how long it took to dissolve. Then she added a second sample of sugar to the hot water, stirred the liquid and timed how long this took to dissolve. By comparing the times she thought she could see whether the temperature of the water *did* affect how quickly the sugar dissolved.

Helen thought she could see what effect temperature had on dissolving, but she had not designed a fair test.

1 Why do you think this is not a fair test?

....

....

National Curriculum links
■ Experimental and investigative work
To be working at level 4 you need to show that you can conduct an investigation fairly.

Links with the Classbook

Unit 52
pages 110–111

Helen had *not* designed a fair test. The temperature of the water was not the **only** difference between the two parts of the investigation.

The different factors which might affect an experiment are called **variables**. If one sample of sugar dissolved quicker than the other sample, Helen would not know whether it was due to the difference in temperature or some other variable.

Now it's your turn

2 Compare the two parts of Helen's investigation by completing the table below:

Variable	Experiment A	Experiment B
container used		
mass of sugar		
volume of water		

3 Are there any other variables which Helen did not keep the same in her investigation?

Write these down in the space below.

....

....

....

National Curriculum links
- ■ Experimental and investigative work
- ■ Planning experimental work

To be working at level 4 you need to show that you can conduct an Investigation fairly.

Links with the Classbook

Unit 52
pages 110–111

When you do an investigation involving a simple comparison you must make sure the only **variable** that you alter is the one that you are investigating. So, you must only change one variable and **control** all the others, by keeping them the same.

Example

In the example shown in *Fair testing 1* (Unit 5), Helen was investigating the effect of changing temperature. She should have changed the temperature and also made sure all the other variables were kept the same (**controlled**). She should have made sure that the size and type of container was the same, the same mass of sugar was used, that the same volume of water was used and that she stirred at the same rate.

John is investigating a completely different topic. He has asked the question:

■ Is 'Sparklo' washing powder better than 'Gleamo'?

John set up his investigation like this:

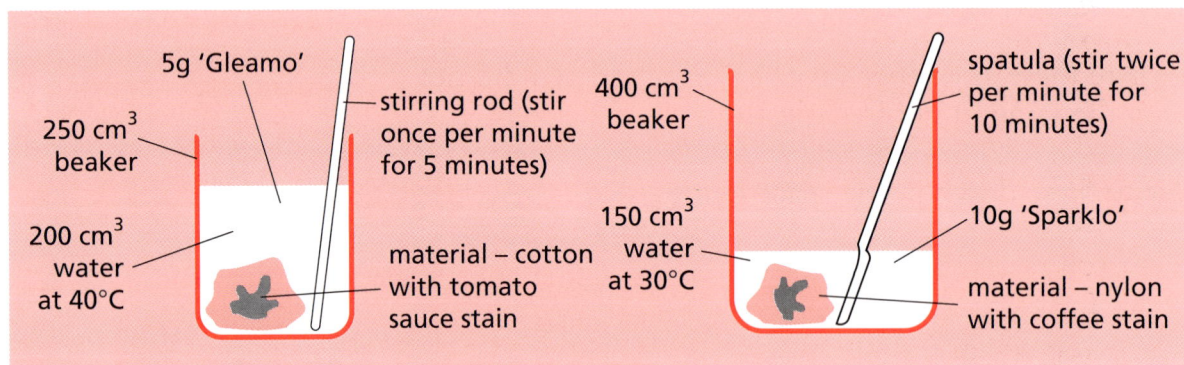

5g 'Gleamo'

250 cm³ beaker

stirring rod (stir once per minute for 5 minutes)

200 cm³ water at 40°C

material – cotton with tomato sauce stain

400 cm³ beaker

spatula (stir twice per minute for 10 minutes)

150 cm³ water at 30°C

10g 'Sparklo'

material – nylon with coffee stain

1 On the diagram, underline in red the variable that John is investigating.

National Curriculum links

■ Experimental and investigative work

■ Planning experimental work

To be working at level 4 you need to show that you can conduct an investigation fairly.

Links with the Classbook

Unit 52
pages 110–111

2 On the diagram opposite, try to underline in blue all the other variables you think he has controlled. Why is this difficult?

....

Now it's your turn

3 In groups, discuss how you think John should have done his investigation.

4 In the space below, draw two labelled diagrams that show how your group thinks John should have performed a fair test.

5 Underline in red the variable you think John is investigating.

6 Now underline in blue all the other variables you decided John should have controlled.

National Curriculum links
- Experimental and investigative work
- Planning experimental work

To be working at level 4 you need to show that you can conduct an investigation fairly.

Links with the Classbook

Unit 52
pages 110–111

In *Fair testing 1* (Unit 5) the effect of changing the temperature was being investigated. However, only two different temperatures were used. With just two results it is difficult to see any **patterns** or **relationships**. We need to improve this by obtaining a **range** of results.

Example

Five different experiments could have been performed at the following temperatures:

- 20 °C
- 30 °C
- 40 °C
- 50 °C
- 60 °C

To show the five different results we would need to design a table. We would also be able to plot a graph of the results to see if there are any patterns or relationships.

Now it's your turn

In *Asking questions* (Unit 2) one suggestion Dafydd made was to see if:

- Beakers with insulation lose heat faster than beakers without insulation.

1 In your groups discuss the questions below:

a How could he improve his investigation so that he has a range of results?

b How many different experiments will he need to do to get a range?

c What will he need to vary when he sets up each experiment?

d What will he need to keep the same when he sets up each experiment?

National Curriculum links

- Experimental and investigative work
- Planning experimental work

To be working at levels 5–8 you will need to design investigations which have a series of observations or measurements.

Links with the Classbook

Unit 50
pages 106–107

Unit 114
pages 238–239

You have discussed how to improve Dafydd's investigation.
Now you are going to write down your thoughts.

2 In the space below, draw a series of diagrams, to show how you think Dafydd should have done his investigation.

3 What could he have used to measure the amount of insulation he put around each beaker?

....

....

National Curriculum links
- Experimental and investigative work
- Planning experimental work

To be working at levels 5–8 you will need to design investigations which have a series of observations or measurements.

Links with the Classbook

Unit 50
pages 106–107

Unit 114
pages 238–239

Sometimes when looking at plants and animals, particularly if they are outside, it is not possible to make a test completely fair. This is because you cannot control every variable you might want to. Many different things can affect the behaviour of animals, or the growth of plants. When you are doing fieldwork it is important to:

- Think what factors could affect the plants, or animals you are studying.

- Identify those things you would like to keep the same but are not able to.

- Try to find a way to measure or compare these factors if you can.

- Collect enough results, from different situations if necessary, so that you can be confident about any conclusions you make.

Example

Nadim and Rose were investigating the question:

- Do snails prefer geraniums or sage plants for food?

1 They looked in the garden and thought that more snails were on the geranium plants. They decided to do the following things to make their investigation better. Underneath each point write down **why** you think they did it.

a They looked at five geranium plants and five sage plants growing in different parts of the garden, some in shade, and some in damp places.

....

b They counted the number of snails on ten leaves of each plant.

....

c They looked carefully and recorded how many snails were actually eating the leaves.

....

National Curriculum links
- Experimental and investigative work
- Planning experimental work

To be working at level 6 you should use scientific knowledge and understanding to identify key factors you need to consider when planning an investigation.

Links with the Classbook

Unit 32
pages 66–67

Now it's your turn

You noticed that two blue tits visit the bird feeders outside the classroom window and that they seem to go to the one containing peanuts more than the one containing sunflower seeds.

You decide to investigate the question:

■ Do blue tits prefer peanuts or sunflower seeds for food?

2 In the space below write down **three** things you would build into the design of your investigation that would help you to answer the question with certainty. *Clue:* What will you measure and how many results will you take?

3 By each of your three points explain **why** you have decided to do this.

1

why?

2

why?

3

why?

National Curriculum links
■ Experimental and investigative work
■ Planning experimental work
To be working at level 6 you should use scientific knowledge and understanding to identify key factors you need to consider when planning an investigation.

Links with the Classbook
Unit 32
pages 66–67

When you perform investigations you will have to make measurements.

You will need to measure:

- the variable which you have chosen to alter
- the variable which gives you the results in your investigation
- all the variables you have controlled to make sure they stay the same.

Example

Imagine you wanted to investigate whether the number of batteries (cells) in a circuit affected the current. You would set up a test circuit and then have to take measurements.

a The variable you have chosen to alter is the number of batteries.

b The variable which gives you the results in your investigation is the current.

c The variables you have controlled are factors such as the other components of the circuit.

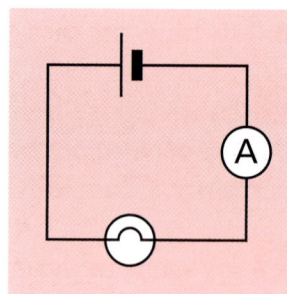

Now it's your turn

1 Describe how you would measure the variable mentioned in (a) above.

2 Describe how you would measure the variable mentioned in (b) above.

3 List **three** of the components of the circuit you would have to keep the same.

National Curriculum links
- Experimental and investigative work
- Planning experimental work

To be working at levels 3–8 you will need to select and use appropriate measuring instruments.

Links with the Classbook

Unit 103
pages 216–217

Unit 104
pages 218–219

It is very important to choose the right measuring instrument for your investigation.

1 The list on the left shows 14 measuring instruments you are likely to use in Science. The list on the right shows a number of things you are likely to measure. Use a ruler to draw a line from the dot by the thing you are measuring to the dot by the measuring instrument you would use to measure it.

Instruments	Things to measure
ammeter •	• angle of a reflected light ray
bathroom scales •	• electrical current
decibel meter •	• electrical voltage
electronic balance •	• force of friction
Newton meter •	• how loud you can shout
$10\,cm^3$ measuring cylinder •	• length of a butterfly
protractor •	• length of the laboratory
pulse monitor •	• temperature of a sample of water
ruler •	• 3.2 g of sugar
tape measure •	• $76\,cm^3$ of water
$100\,cm^3$ measuring cylinder •	• 112 g of aluminium
thermometer •	• your heart rate
triple beam balance •	• your weight
voltmeter •	• $6\,cm^3$ of water

2 Explain why you would choose a different instrument to measure 3.2 g of sugar and your weight.

....

....

3 Explain why you would choose a different instrument to measure $6\,cm^3$ of water and $76\,cm^3$ of water.

....

....

National Curriculum links
- Experimental and investigative work
- Planning experimental work

To be working at levels 3–8 you will need to select and use appropriate measuring instruments.

Links with the Classbook
There are many links including **Forces** *starting on page 164,* **Electricity and magnetism** *from page 210,* **Unit 51** *pages 108–109 and* **Unit 53** *pages 112–113.*

Obtaining Evidence

This diagram shows the important ideas you will cover in this section.

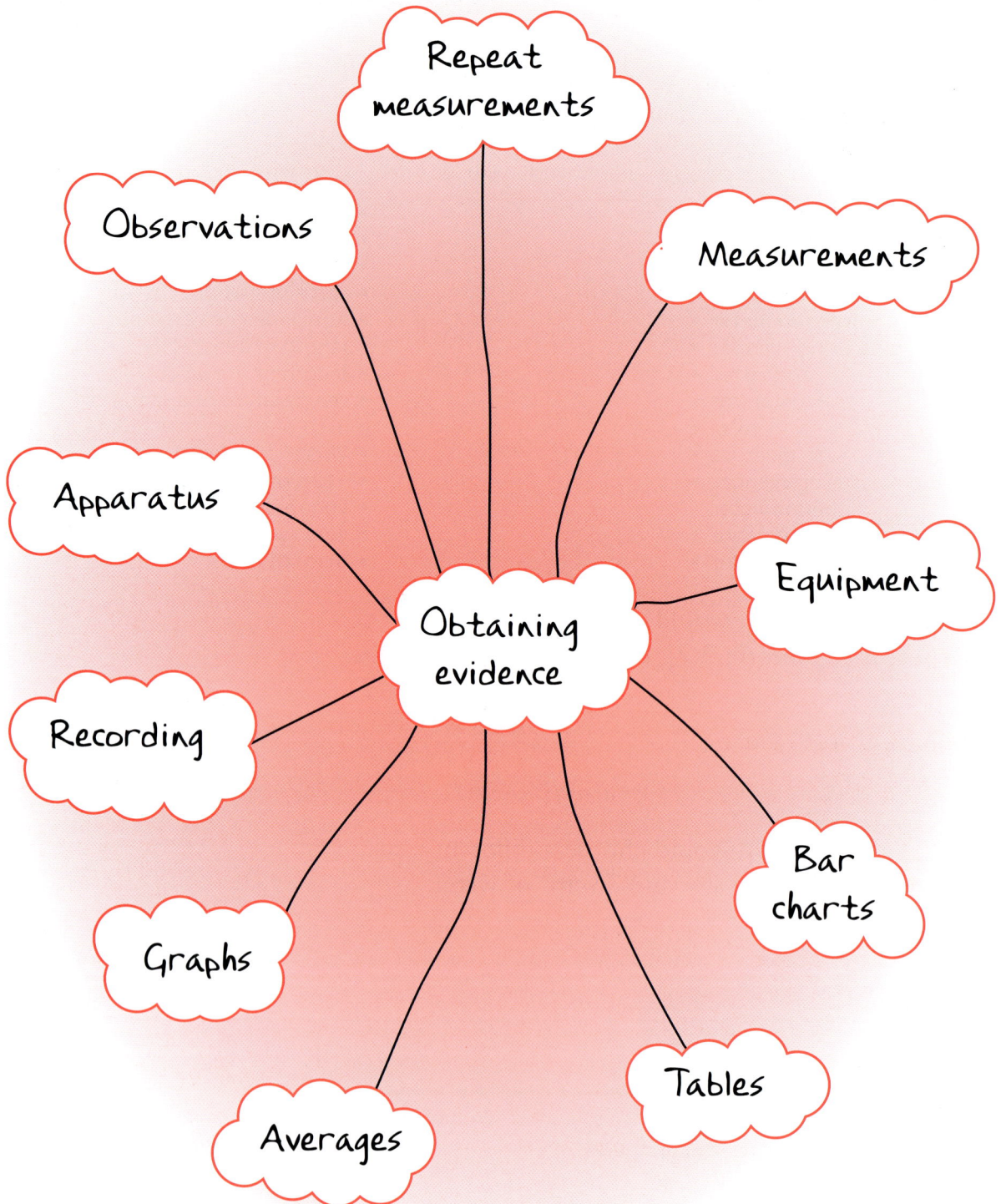

Repeat measurements

Observations

Measurements

Apparatus

Obtaining evidence

Equipment

Recording

Bar charts

Graphs

Tables

Averages

Improving my ability to obtain evidence

Again, as you work through the book you will pick up tips and ideas. When you find something which helps you to **improve how you obtain evidence,** write it down in the spaces below.

There are **five** main areas that you should cover when you are obtaining evidence. These are:

1 How do I use a range of apparatus and equipment safely and with skill?

....

....

2 How do I make observations and measurements with enough precision for the investigation I am doing?

....

....

3 How many observations and measurements do I need to make to produce reliable evidence?

....

....

4 When should I repeat observations and measurements?

....

....

5 How do I record my evidence clearly and appropriately as I carry out my work?

....

....

Having chosen the appropriate measuring instrument (Unit 10), you need to know how to read the scale accurately.

Taking an accurate reading can be done in **six** steps:

1 Find where your reading is on the scale.

2 Work out what the two main numbers are either side of your reading.

3 Count how many divisions there are between the main numbers.

4 Work out the value of each division.

5 Work out the reading.

6 Don't forget the unit.

Example

Look at the thermometer shown on the right. The top of the liquid is between two main numbers, 20°C and 30°C. There are ten divisions between these two main numbers, so each division equals 1°C. Therefore, the thermometer is reading 26°C.

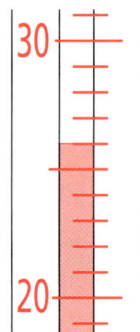

Now it's your turn

1 For each of the scales below work through the six steps above and write down the reading on the scale.

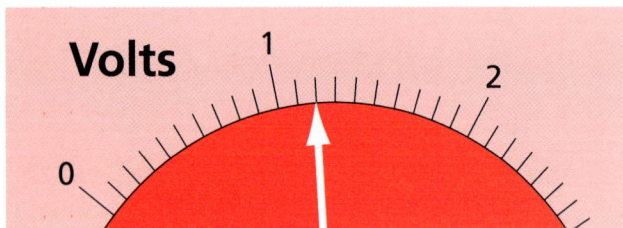

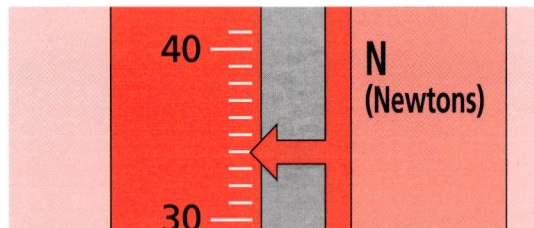

Volts

N (Newtons)

a What current does the ammeter read? ....

b What force does the forcemeter read? ....

National Curriculum links

- Experimental and investigative work
- Obtaining evidence

To be working at levels 3–8 you will need to make measurements with precision appropriate to the task.

Links with the Classbook

Unit 111
pages 232–233

2 What is the length of the line?

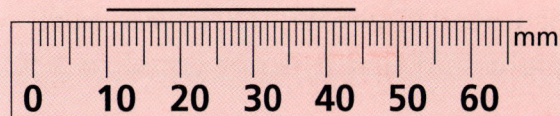

....

3 What temperature does thermometer A show?

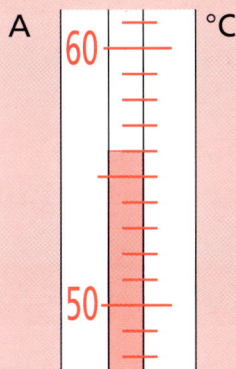

....

4 What temperature does thermometer B show?

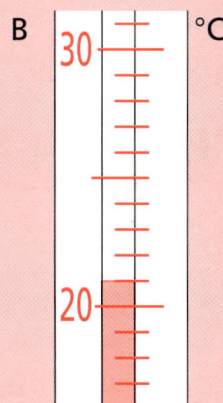

....

5 What volume of water is in measuring cylinder A?

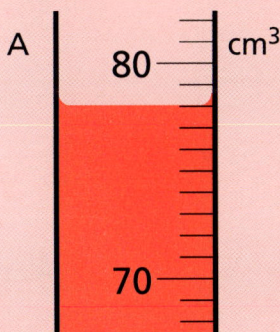

....

6 What volume of water is in measuring cylinder B?

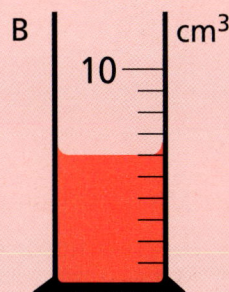

....

mm

0 10 20 30 40 50 60

A °C
60

50

B °C
30

20

A cm³
80

70

B cm³
10

National Curriculum links
- Experimental and investigative work
- Obtaining evidence

To be working at levels 3–8 you will need to make measurements with precision appropriate to the task.

Links with the Classbook
Unit 111
pages 232–233

You can use the six steps shown in *Reading scales 1* (Unit 12) for all scales. However, when you work out the value of a division you might find that it is not equal to 1 °C, 1 cm or 1 g.

Example

There are other possible values for a division. For example:

■ If there are 10 divisions between 6 A and 7 A on an ammeter, then one division equals 0.1 A.

■ If there are only 5 divisions between 40 °C and 50 °C on a thermometer, then one division equals 2 °C.

Now it's your turn

1 For each of the scales below work through the six steps shown in *Reading scales 1* and write down the reading on the scale.

   a What temperature does thermometer A show?

   b What temperature does thermometer B show?

   c What temperature does thermometer C show?

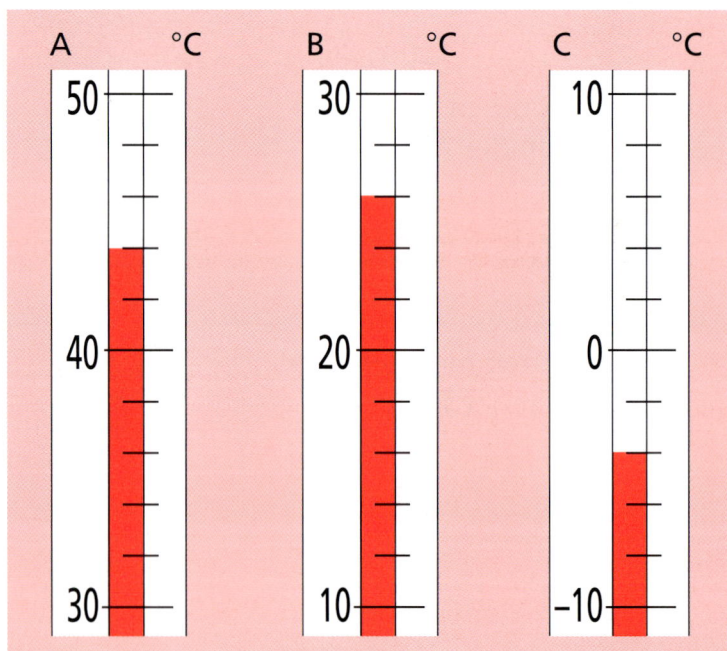

National Curriculum links
■ Experimental and investigative work
■ Obtaining evidence
To be working at levels 3–8 you will need to make measurements with precision appropriate to the task.

Links with the Classbook
Unit 111
pages 232–233

2 To give you practice here are some more scales. Watch out – some are unusual!

a What force does the forcemeter A show?

....

b What voltage does the voltmeter B show?

....

c What length is the line C?

....

d What voltage does the voltmeter D show?

....

e What mass does the balance E show?

....

f What volume of water is in the measuring cylinder F?

....

A

80

70

60

N (Newtons)

B

2

3

4

1

5

**V
(Volts)**

C

5

4

3

2

1

0

cm

D

2

3

1

**V
(Volts)**

E

1

2

g (grams)

F

9

8

7

cm³

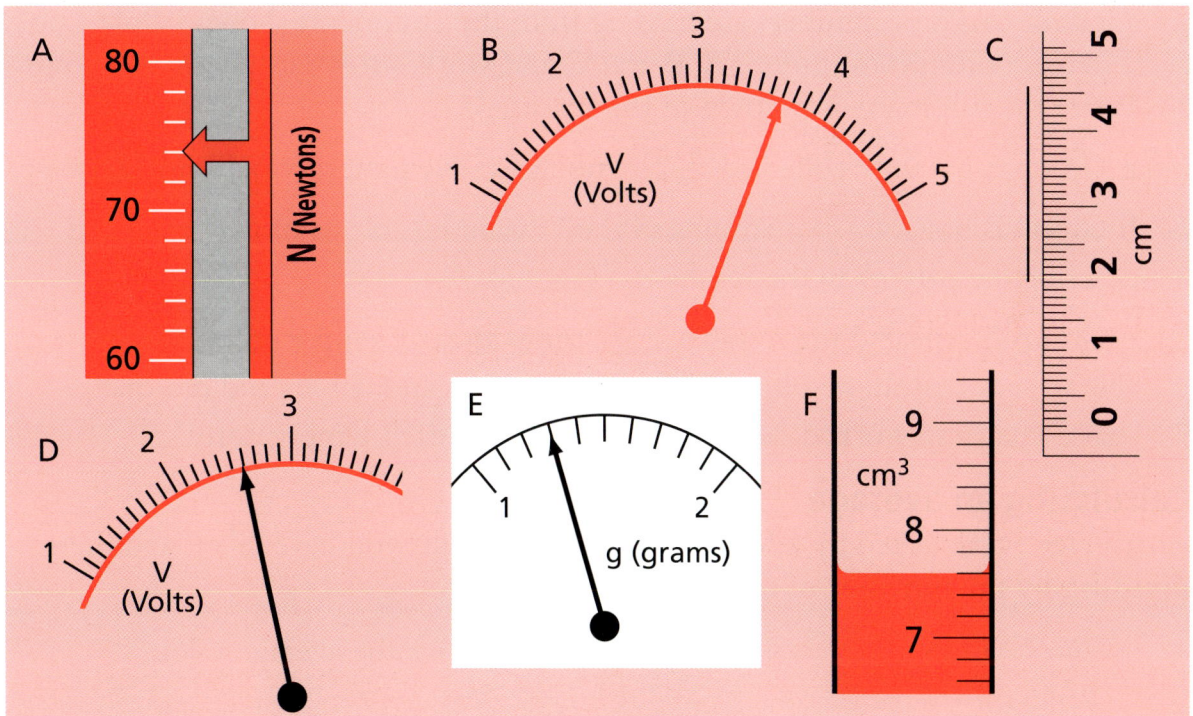

National Curriculum links

■ Experimental and investigative work

■ Obtaining evidence

*To be working at levels 3–8 you will need to make measurements
with precision appropriate to the task.*

**Links with the
Classbook**

Unit 104
pages 218–219

When you plan an investigation it is important to think about the number of results you are going to collect. You should aim to collect enough information to show any patterns in the results.

It is sometimes useful to repeat results and work out an average. This will help to highlight any results that are odd because something went wrong during the investigation. Results that are odd and don't fit in with the rest are called **anomalous results**. Working out an average also evens out any small differences in results.

Example

Groups of pupils were investigating the question:

■ Does the temperature of water affect how long it takes sugar to dissolve?

Three sets of results are shown on the page opposite.

1   Certain words or numbers are missing from the comments shown below. Look at the tables of results for groups A, B and C and work out what the missing words are. Write the missing words down in the spaces.

   a Group A has only collected ⬚⬚⬚⬚ results so any pattern would not show up.

   b Group B has got ⬚⬚⬚⬚ results so they would be able to plot a graph and describe the pattern in the results.

   c Group C repeated the results ⬚⬚⬚⬚ times at each temperature. They were able to spot that the result of ⬚⬚⬚⬚ minutes was anomalous and did that test again. They also worked out ⬚⬚⬚⬚⬚⬚⬚ for each temperature.

Calculating an average

An average is calculated by **adding** together the results you have taken and then **dividing** by the **number** of results you have taken.

    ■ 6+7+5=18   ■ 18÷3 = 6   ■ so 6 is the average value

National Curriculum links
■ Experimental and investigative work
■ Obtaining evidence

To be working at levels 5–8 you need to know when you have made enough observations or measurements and when to repeat these to get reliable data.

Links with the Classbook

Unit 22
pages 46–47

Group A

Temperature (°C)	Time (mins)
20	8
50	4

Group B

Temperature (°C)	Time (mins)
20	8
30	6
40	5
50	4
60	3

Group C

Temperature (°C)	Time			
	Time 1	Time 2	Time 3	Average
20	8	8	~~17~~ 8	8
30	6	7	5	6
40	5	5	4	4.7
50	4	4	4	4
60	3	3	3	3

anomalous result

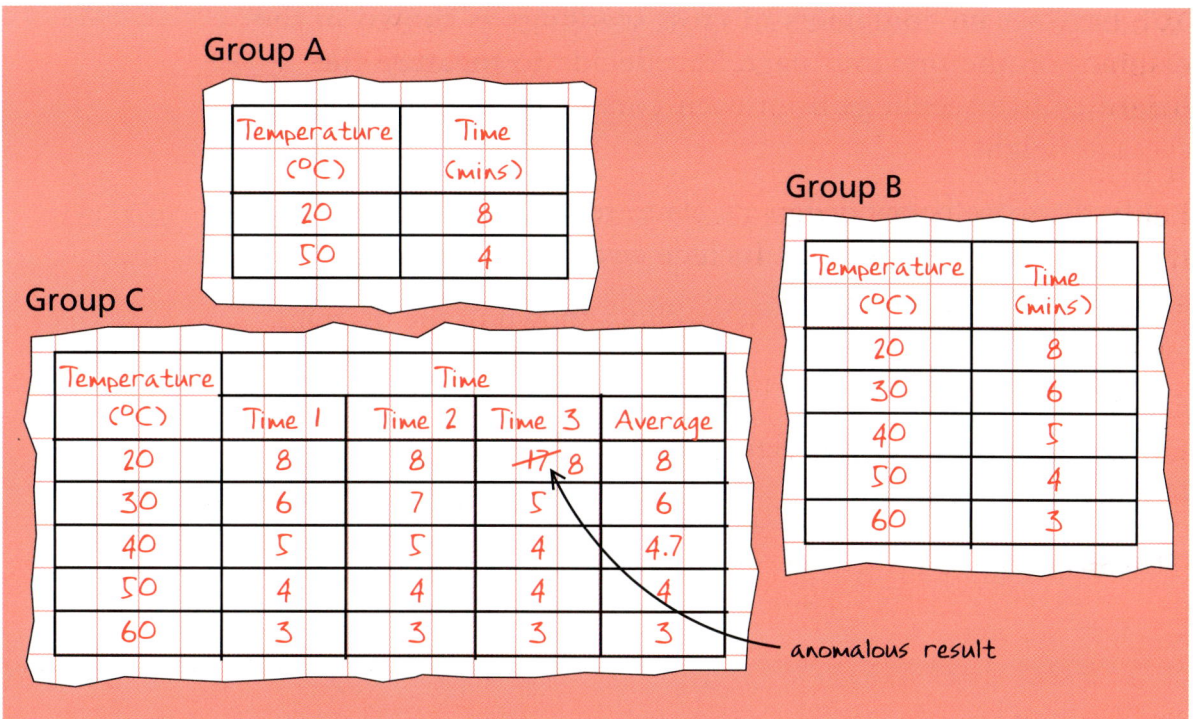

Now it's your turn

You are investigating the question:

■ Does the amount of light affect how cress seedlings grow?

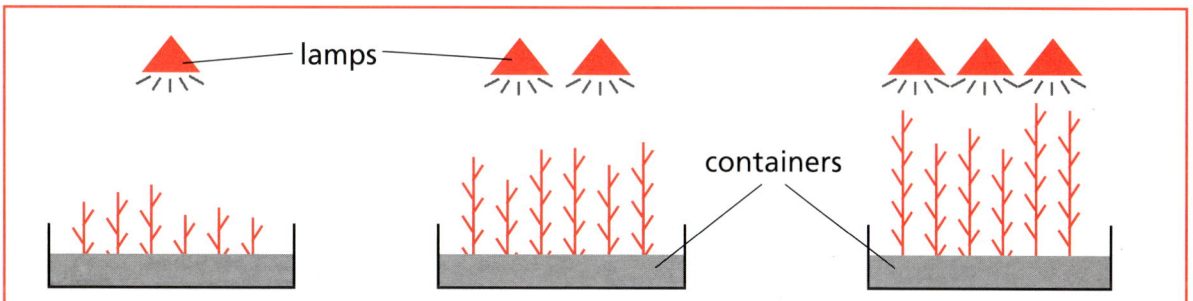

lamps

containers

National Curriculum links

■ Experimental and investigative work
■ Obtaining evidence

To be working at levels 5–8 you need to know when you have made enough observations or measurements and when to repeat these to get reliable data.

continued...

Links with the Classbook

Unit 22
pages 46–47

You have set up containers of cress seedlings as shown in the diagram on the previous page. You decide to measure the height of five seedlings from each container and work out the average height.

2 In the space below design a table to record the complete set of results from this investigation. Include any averages in your table.

3 Carefully measure all fifteen seedlings shown in the diagram.

4 Add these results to your table.

5 Work out the average height of the seedlings and add these results to your table.

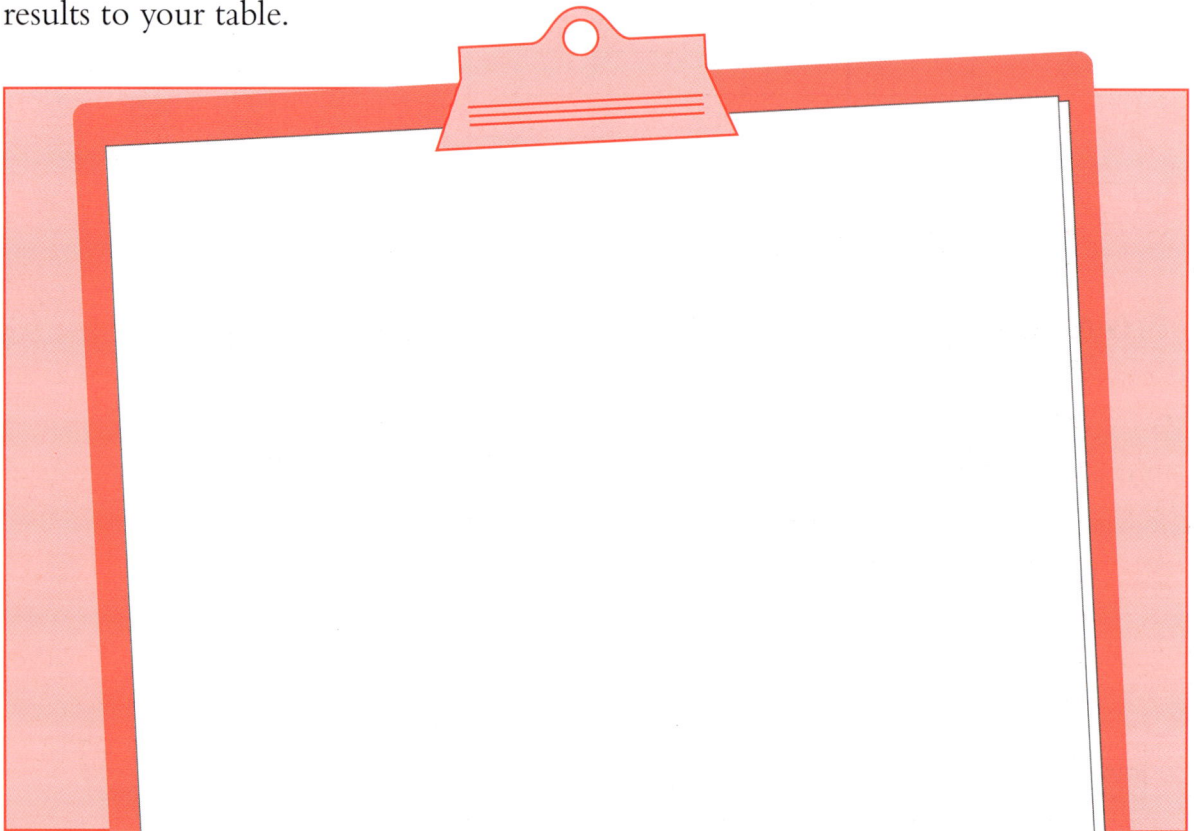

National Curriculum links
- Experimental and investigative work
- Obtaining evidence

To be working at levels 5–8 you need to know when you have made enough observations or measurements and when to repeat these to get reliable data.

Links with the Classbook
Unit 22
pages 46–47

You are now at the stage of doing your investigation and collecting results. It is important to lay out your results in a neat and organised way so that they are easily understood. A good table will make it easier for you to plot a graph of your results.

Example

The title of the variable you are changing. (This goes in the first column of your table.)

The title for the variable you are investigating. (This goes in the second column of your table.)

The unit for this variable.

The unit for this variable.

The results in the table do not need any units since they are shown at the top of the table.

Now it's your turn

Jack was investigating whether the height of one end of a ramp affected the time it took for a car to roll down the ramp. He scribbled down his results in the back of his Science book. Jack had not thought through how he was going to record the results.

1 Transfer Jack's results into the example table above.

time to roll down 12 sec
height of ramp 10 cm

time to roll down 6 sec
height 10 cm

time to roll down 10 sec
height 10 cm

time to roll down 4 sec
height 25 cm

National Curriculum links
- Experimental and investigative work
- Obtaining evidence

To be working at levels 4–8 you should be able to organise your results into tables.

Links with the Classbook

Unit 77
pages 164–165

Analysing evidence and drawing conclusions

This diagram shows the important ideas you will cover in this section.

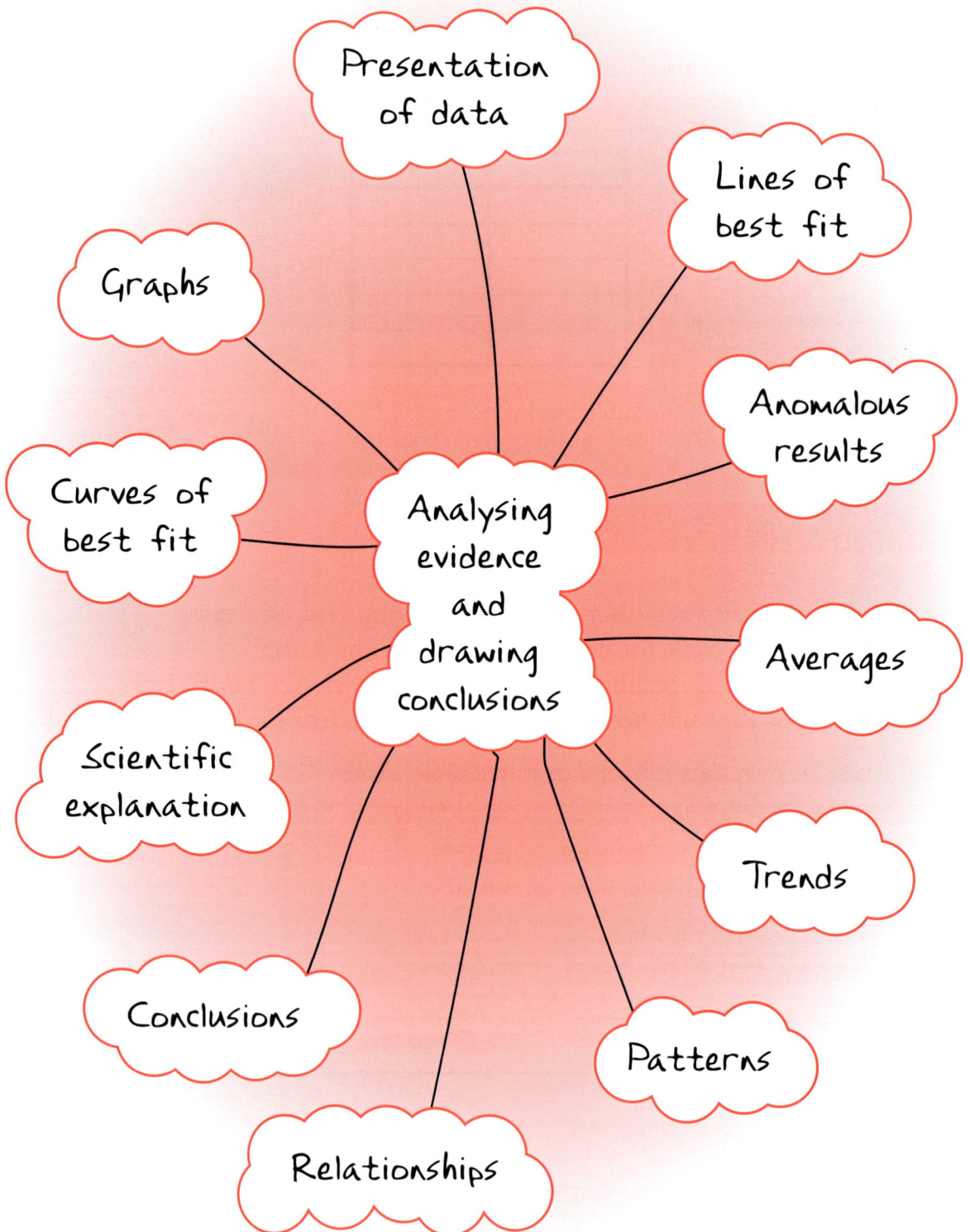

Presentation of data

Lines of best fit

Graphs

Anomalous results

Curves of best fit

Analysing evidence and drawing conclusions

Averages

Scientific explanation

Trends

Conclusions

Patterns

Relationships

Improving how I analyse evidence and draw conclusions

Again, as you work through the book you will pick up tips and ideas. When you find something which helps you to **improve the way you analyse evidence and draw conclusions,** write it down in the spaces below.

There are **seven** main areas that you should cover when you are obtaining evidence. These are:

1 How do I draw a graph of my results?

2 How do I use lines and curves of best fit?

3 What words do I use to describe trends or patterns in results?

4 What is the difference between qualitative and quantitative data?

5 How do I present qualitative data?

6 How do I present quantitative data?

7 What do I need to say in a conclusion?

Sometimes when you collect results they fall into **categories** or **types** rather than having a value which you have measured. Bar charts can be a useful way of showing these results.

Example

Imagine you had investigated the question:

■ Which types of bird visit the nut feeder most frequently?

A bar chart of your results could look like the one on the right.

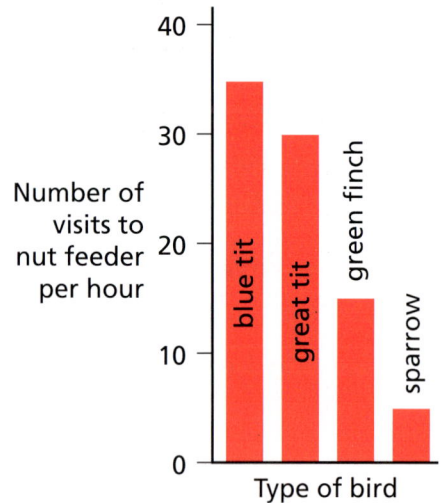

Number of visits to nut feeder per hour

Type of bird

Now it's your turn

Karen and Yusif have decided to light different candles, cover them with a beaker and time how long it takes for them to go out. They asked the question:

■ Does the type of candle affect how long it burns?

The results they collected are shown in the table below.

1   Draw a bar chart of the results in the space provided.

Type of candle	Time to go out (seconds)
night light	30
birthday	7
standard	18
long life	25
sailor's friend (edible!)	2

National Curriculum links
■ Experimental and investigative work
■ Analysing evidence and drawing conclusions

To be working at level 4 you must be able to present information clearly using bar charts.

Links with the Classbook

Unit 66
pages 138–139

As you saw in *Tables of results* (Unit 15), Jack collected a set of results for a car rolling down a ramp. However, it isn't easy to see a pattern or relationship even though he has organised his results into a table. Jack must plot a graph of the results to see any patterns that might exist. It is important to know how to plot a graph correctly.

Example Here is a graph of the results from an experiment like Jack's.

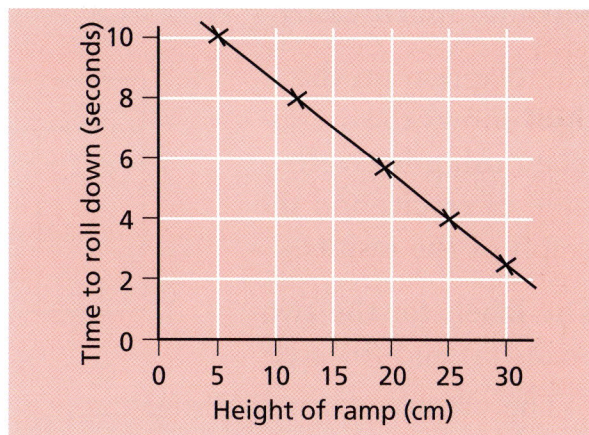

Now it's your turn

To draw a good graph it helps to follow certain rules.

1 Use the words below to fill in the blanks and complete the rules.

anomalous   axes   best   correctly   numbers   paper   scales   unit

To draw a graph to make sure that:

a the .... are the correct way round

b the axes are labelled with a title and a ....

c the scales have .... that are evenly spaced out

d the .... for the axes are appropriate for the results

e the graph uses as much of the graph .... as possible

f the points are plotted ....

g a line or curve of .... fit has been estimated and drawn accurately

h .... results are ignored.

National Curriculum links
- Experimental and investigative work
- Analysing evidence and drawing conclusions

To be working at levels 4–8 you should be able to plot line graphs correctly.

Links with the Classbook

Unit 52
pages 110–111

Unit 78
pages 166–167

There is a close relationship between a table of results and a graph. If you have laid out your table correctly then plotting a graph becomes much easier.

The diagram on the right shows the relationship between a table of results and the graph of the results.

The labels for the two boxes (a) and (b) are:

- The variable you are investigating (e.g. height of the ramp)
- The variable that changes as a result of your experiment (e.g. time to roll down)

1 Decide which label goes in which box and then write them in.

Let's look at this relationship with a new experiment. Jamie is looking at how magnesium reacts with acid. He is investigating whether or not the temperature of the acid will change how quickly the reaction takes place. Jamie has plotted a graph but he has not done it very well. This is the table of results he was working from and his poor attempt at a graph.

Temperature of the acid (°C)	Time for the magnesium to disappear (secs)
10	60
20	20
30	10
40	5
50	2

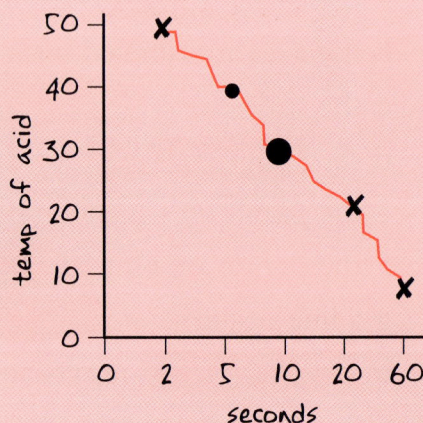

National Curriculum links
- Experimental and investigative work
- Analysing evidence and drawing conclusions

To be working at levels 4–8 you should be able to plot line graphs correctly.

Links with the Classbook
Unit 68
pages 142–143

Now it's your turn

Look at the example of a good graph in *Graphs 1* (Unit 18) and
compare this with Jamie's graph.

2 There are at least seven ways in which Jamie's graph could be improved.
In the space below make a list of these improvements:

....

....

....

....

....

3 Use your list of
improvements to plot your
own graph of Jamie's results.

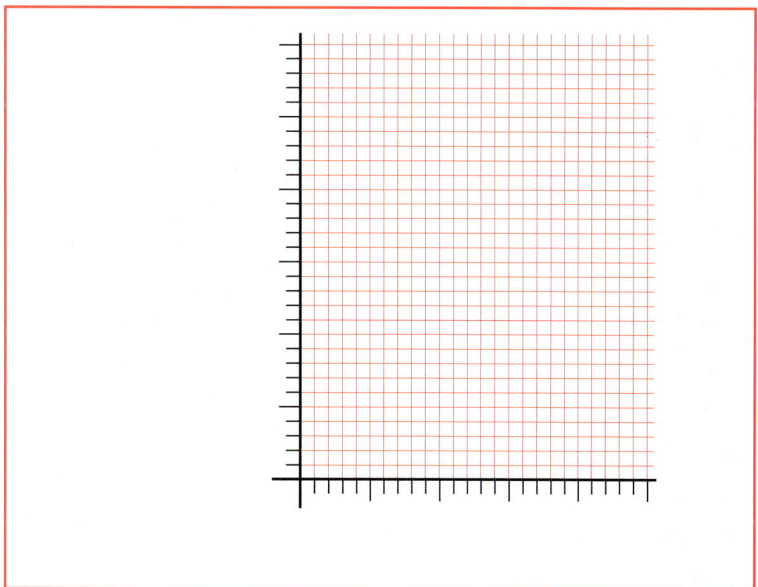

National Curriculum links
■ Experimental and investigative work
■ Analysing evidence and drawing conclusions
*To be working at levels 4–8 you should be able to plot line graphs
correctly.*

**Links with the
Classbook**
Unit 68
pages 142–143

Take a moment to think through what you have learned about graphs. Remember, it's important when plotting a graph to make sure that:

■ The axes are the correct way round (see *Graphs 1*, Unit 18)

■ Your results are plotted to fill as much of the graph paper as possible. (A scale doesn't necessarily have to start at zero.)

■ The divisions on the scale are equal.

Example

Beatrice and two of her friends (Mark and Ben) were doing a similar experiment to Jamie's. They added different lengths of magnesium ribbon to dilute hydrochloric acid. They timed how long it took for the magnesium to react and disappear. Here is their table of results:

Length of magnesium (cm)	Time taken to react (secs)
1	36
2	45
3	51
4	55
5	60

Each of the three friends plotted a graph of the results to see if there was a relationship between the length of the magnesium ribbon and the time taken to react. Here are their attempts at plotting the graphs:

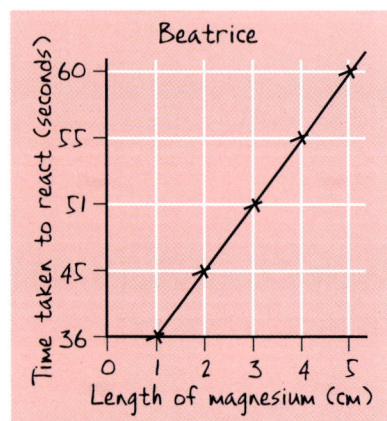

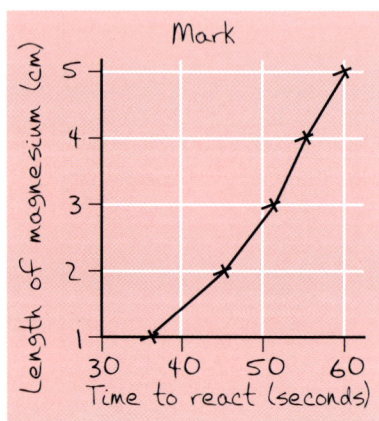

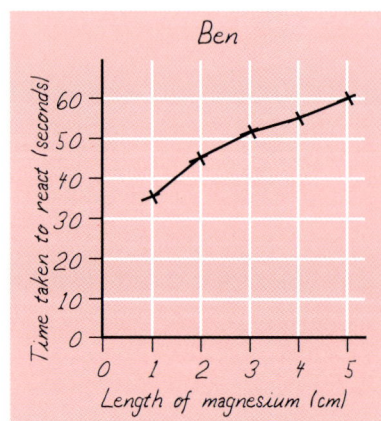

Beatrice — Time taken to react (seconds) vs Length of magnesium (cm)

Mark — Length of magnesium (cm) vs Time to react (seconds)

Ben — Time taken to react (seconds) vs Length of magnesium (cm)

National Curriculum links
■ Experimental and investigative work
■ Analysing evidence and drawing conclusions

To be working at levels 4–8 you should be able to plot line graphs correctly.

Links with the Classbook

Unit 68
pages 142–143

Now it's your turn

Beatrice and her two friends have made mistakes with each of their graphs.

1 Look carefully at the graphs and then write down the mistakes that each of them has made.

Beatrice ....

Mark ....

Ben ....

2 Having decided what mistakes they made, plot a correct graph of the results on the graph paper below.

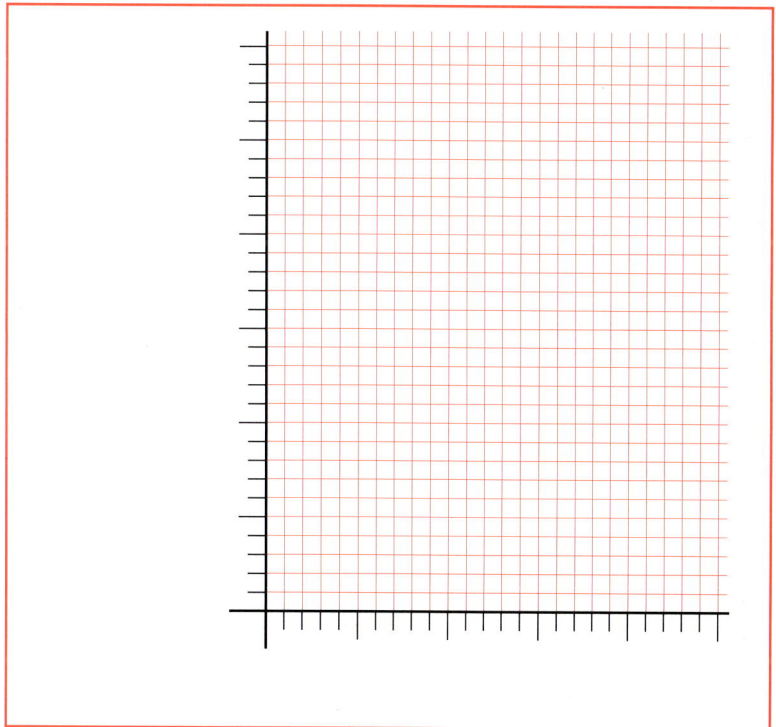

National Curriculum links
- Experimental and investigative work
- Analysing evidence and drawing conclusions

To be working at levels 4–8 you should be able to plot line graphs correctly.

Links with the Classbook

Unit 68
pages 142–143

Often when you collect the results from an investigation and plot a graph the points do not lie in a perfect straight line. This could be due to small variations or errors as you collected the results. It could be that the results are true and shouldn't lie in a straight line!

If you are sure that the results should be in a straight line then you can draw a **line of best fit**. This is a line that goes through, or close to, as many of the points as possible.

If one result is a long way from the line it is probably an **anomalous result** – one where something went wrong in the investigation. It is best to leave out this result when drawing the line.

Force (N)	Stretch of spring (cm)
2	2.0
4	4.1
6	6.0
8	3.5
10	10.2
12	11.9

Example

The table of results on the right and graph shown below are from an investigation to answer the question:

- Does the force on a spring affect how much it stretches?

Notice that the line does not go through every point. One result is a long way from the line.

1 What name is given to this type of result?

....

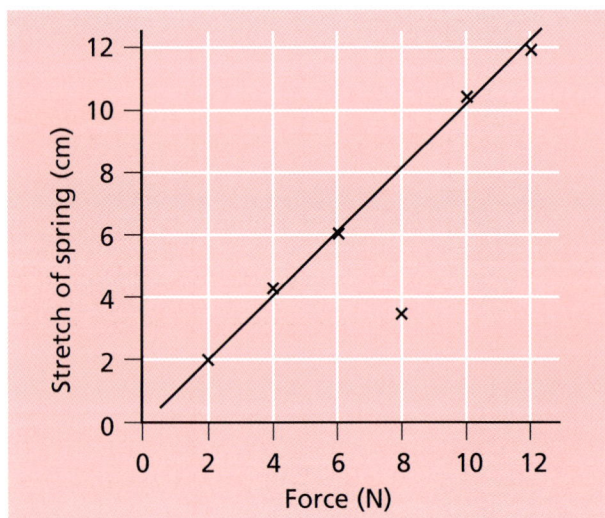

National Curriculum links
- Experimental and investigative work
- Analysing evidence and drawing conclusions

To be working at levels 6–7 you should be able to draw lines of best fit and identify anomalous results.

Links with the Classbook

Unit 79
pages 168–169

Now it's your turn

The results shown on the right are from another investigation to answer the same question.

Force (N)	Extension (cm)
1	3.5
2	7.1
3	10.3
4	12.0
5	17.5
6	20.8

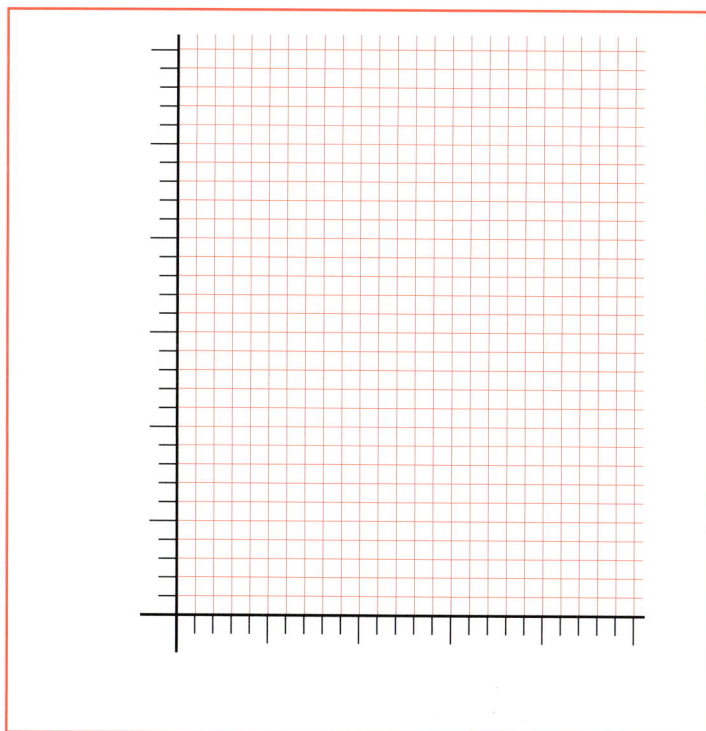

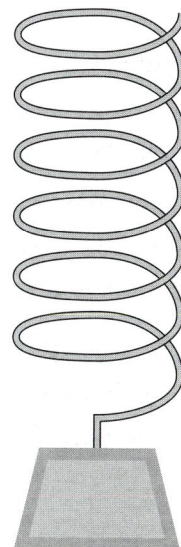

2 Plot the results on the graph paper below and draw in a line of best fit.

3 Label any anomalous results.

National Curriculum links
- Experimental and investigative work
- Analysing evidence and drawing conclusions

To be working at levels 6–7 you should be able to draw lines of best fit and identify anomalous results.

Links with the Classbook
Unit 79
pages 168–169

Graphs 5

The results from an investigation will not always give a straight-line graph. Sometimes the points will form a curve.

If, when you look at the pattern of your results, you think this is the case it is usual to draw a **curve of best fit**. This is a curve which goes through, or close to, as many points as possible but also follows an even curve. Drawing a curve can be tricky so sketch very faintly at first.

Example

The results table on the right and graph shown below are from an investigation to answer the question:

- How does the amount of light available affect the rate of photosynthesis?

Shamim and Steve set up their apparatus as shown in the diagram below. They were able to change the amount of light available by using small lamps. They measured the rate of photosynthesis by counting the number of bubbles of oxygen the pondweed gave off in a minute.

Number of lamps	Number of bubbles per minute
1	4
2	20
3	32
4	36
5	39
6	39

1 Label the diagram of the apparatus and the axes for the graph using the words below:

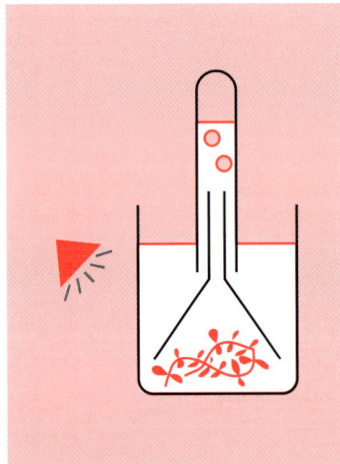

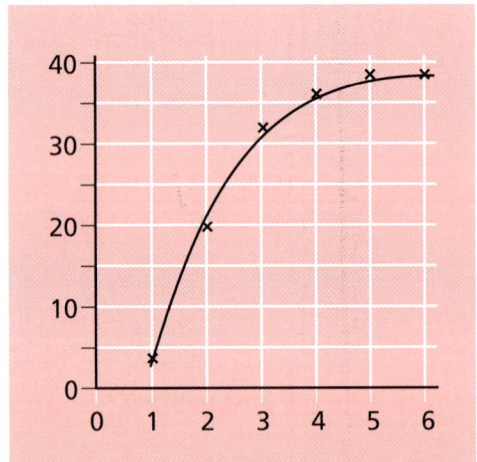

beaker   bubbles of oxygen   lamp   number of bubbles
number of lamps   pondweed

National Curriculum links
- Experimental and investigative work
- Analysing evidence and drawing conclusions

To be working at levels 6–7 you should be able to draw lines of best fit and identify anomalous results.

Links with the Classbook

Unit 22
pages 46–47

Now it's your turn

Another group, also investigating photosynthesis, collected the results below. They were trying to answer the question:

■ How does the temperature of the water affect how quickly pondweed photosynthesises?

The pupils counted the number of bubbles produced per minute but this time the light was kept constant. Only the water temperature was changed.

2 Plot a graph of their results in the space below and draw in the curve of best fit.

Water temperature (°C)	Number of bubbles per minute
5	5
10	17
15	26
20	32
25	35
30	34
35	37

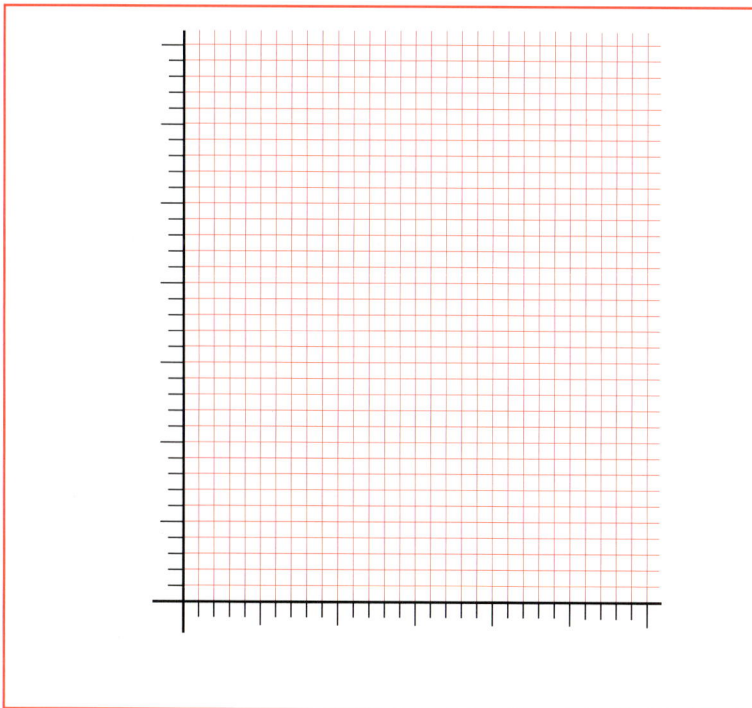

National Curriculum links
■ Experimental and investigative work
■ Analysing evidence and drawing conclusions
To be working at levels 6–7 you should be able to draw lines of best fit and identify anomalous results.

Links with the Classbook

Unit 22
pages 46–47

When you write a conclusion to your investigation the first thing you need to do is to describe the results you have collected. Try to say what effect changing your variable had on the results you got. Try to use the terms 'increase', 'decrease', or 'remains constant'. Remember the variable you are investigating is in the left hand column of your table or along the bottom axis of your graph. The variable that changes as a result is in the right hand column of your table or up the side of your graph.

Examples

Kathy and Russell did an investigation to answer the question:

- How does the temperature of water affect the mass of sugar that will dissolve in it?

A sketch graph of their results is shown here.

They were able to say in their conclusion that:

- As the temperature of the water is increased the amount of sugar that dissolves also increases.

Anton and Alistair were investigating the question:

- What effect does the mass of a pendulum have on the number of swings it makes in a minute?

A sketch graph of their results is shown here.

They were able to say that:

- As the mass of our pendulum was increased the number of swings per minute stayed constant.

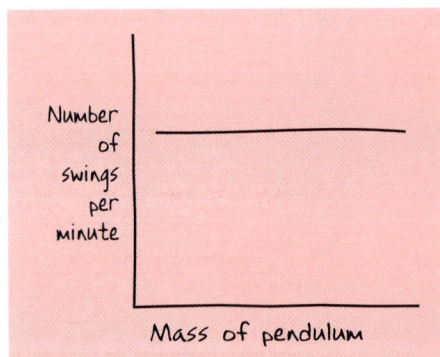

National Curriculum links
- Experimental and investigative work
- Analysing evidence and drawing conclusions

To be working at levels 5–7 you have to be able to write conclusions that are consistent with the results you have collected.

Links with the Classbook

Unit 52
pages 110–111

Unit 79
pages 168–169

Now it's your turn

Next to each of the three graphs shown below write
a sentence which could be used in a conclusion.
The sentence must describe the results.

Question:

■ What effect will
increasing the force
have on the stretch
of a spring?

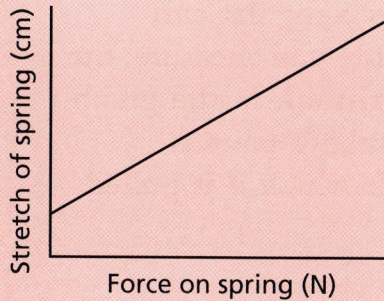

Stretch of spring (cm)

Force on spring (N)

....

....

....

Question:

■ Does increasing the
temperature of water
make sugar dissolve
faster?

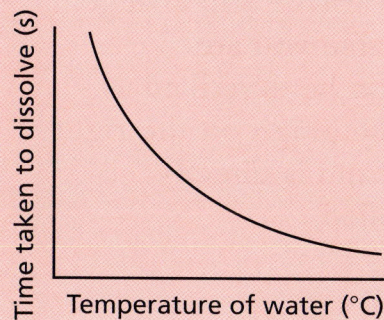

Time taken to dissolve (s)

Temperature of water (°C)

....

....

....

Question:

■ As the amount of
light is increased
what happens
to the rate of
photosynthesis?

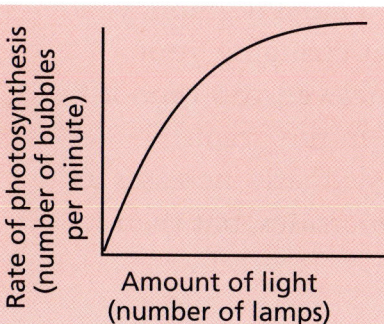

Rate of photosynthesis
(number of bubbles
per minute)

Amount of light
(number of lamps)

....

....

....

National Curriculum links

■ Experimental and investigative work

■ Analysing evidence and drawing conclusions

*To be working at levels 5–7 you have to be able to write
conclusions that are consistent with the results you have collected.*

**Links with the
Classbook**
Unit 22 *pages* 46–47

Unit 52 *pages* 110–111
Unit 79 *pages* 168–169

When you plot a graph, it allows you to look at all the results you have collected and to compare them. Graphs make spotting patterns or trends in your results easier. You need to know what language to use to describe the patterns you see.

Examples

If the variable you change has a regular and increasing effect on the variable you measure, the results are said to be **proportional**. In the graph on the right the length of a rubber band is proportional to the force with which it is pulled.

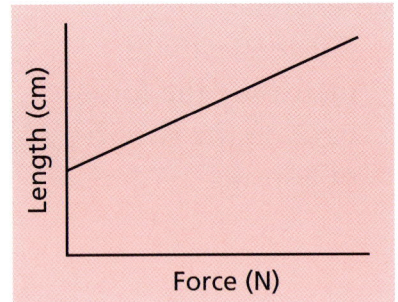

If doubling the value of the variable you change doubles the value of the variable you are measuring, then the results can be described as **directly proportional**. In the graph on the right the extension of the rubber band is directly proportional to the force applied.

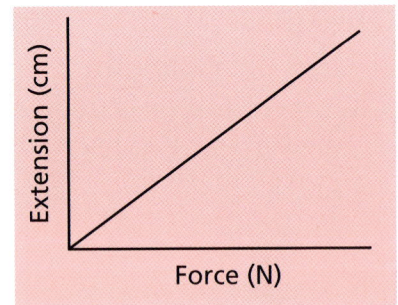

If your investigation produces a curved graph, you can still describe the effect that changing your variable had on the results. However, you cannot say that they are proportional. In the graph on the right the rate of photosynthesis increases as the amount of light available increases, but then it stays constant.

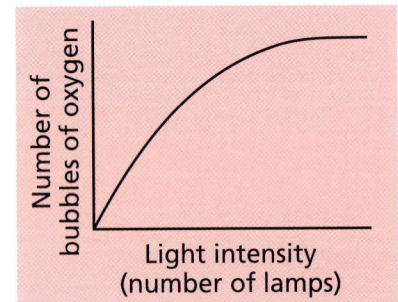

National Curriculum links
- Experimental and investigative work
- Analysing evidence and drawing conclusions

To be working at levels 6–8 you will need to use scientific language to describe your results and graphs.

Links with the Classbook

Unit 22
pages 46–47

Unit 79
pages 168–169

Now it's your turn

1 Write a sentence or short paragraph to describe the pattern of each of the results shown below. To describe the third graph try to combine two ideas from the examples.

Question:
- What effect does the length of a piece of magnesium ribbon have on the time it takes to react in dilute hydrochloric acid?

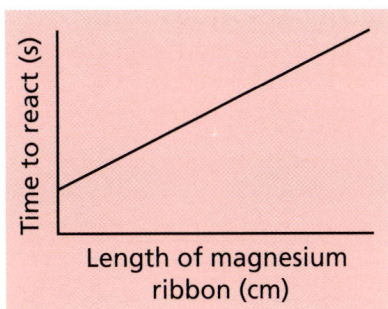

....

....

....

....

Question:
- How does the rate at which pondweed photosynthesises change as water temperature increases?

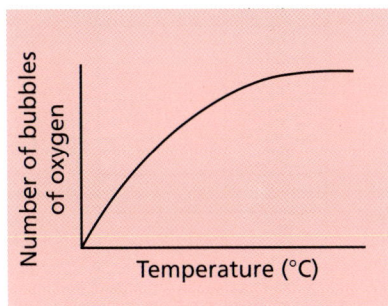

....

....

....

....

Question:
- What happens to the stretch of a spring as the force exerted on it is increased?

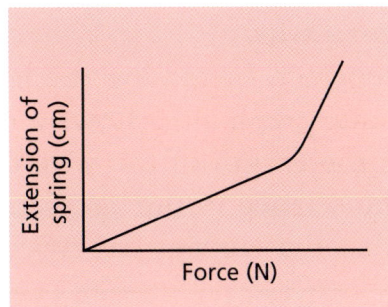

....

....

....

....

National Curriculum links
- Experimental and investigative work
- Analysing evidence and drawing conclusions

To be working at levels 6–8 you will need to use scientific language to describe your results and graphs.

Links with the Classbook

Unit 22 *pages* 46–47
Unit 79 *pages* 168–169

The last activity helped you to spot and describe patterns in your results. However, in your conclusion you also need to explain what the results mean.

You should:
- Link your conclusion back to your prediction.
- Try to give a scientific reason for your conclusion.

Example

Karen and Li were investigating the question:
- What effect will increasing the length of a piece of constantan wire have on its resistance?

They predicted:
Increasing the length of the wire will increase the resistance.

Their scientific idea for this was that:
As the length of the wire is increased, the current has further to flow.

The **table of results** and **graph** they drew are shown on the right.

Length of wire (°C)	Resistance (ohms)
20	10
30	15
40	20
50	25
60	30
70	35
80	40

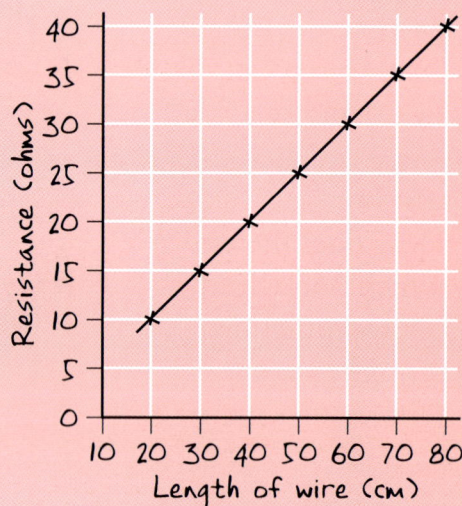

The conclusion they wrote was:
Our prediction was partly correct. Increasing the length of wire does increase the resistance but our graph also shows a directly proportional relationship. As you double the length of the wire the resistance also doubles. This fits in with the science in our prediction because doubling the length of wire means that the current has twice as far to go.

National Curriculum links
- Experimental and investigative work
- Analysing evidence and drawing conclusions

To be working at levels 5–8 you need to make predictions and draw conclusions based on scientific knowledge. Your conclusions should take account of the number of results you have collected and be linked to them.

Links with the Classbook

Unit 104
pages 218–219

Unit 114
pages 238–239

Now it's your turn

1 Look at the investigation on this page and the one on the next page. Write a conclusion for each. Remember, a conclusion should have:

■ a description of the pattern of the results
■ a link to the original prediction
■ a scientific explanation.

Question:

■ Which type of material provides the best heat insulation?

Prediction:

■ Expanded polystyrene will provide the best insulation because it is the lightest material.

Conclusion:

....

....

....

....

....

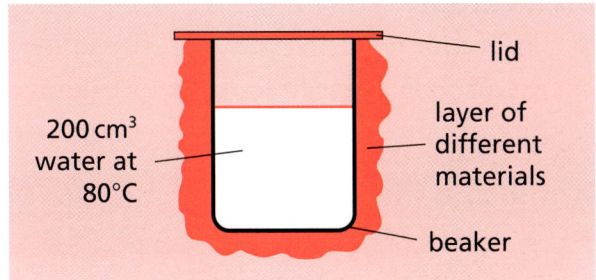

200 cm³ water at 80°C

lid

layer of different materials

beaker

Results:

Type of material	Temperature after 15 mins (°C)
wood	50
expanded polystyrene	55
aluminium	40
clay tile	44
polythene	50

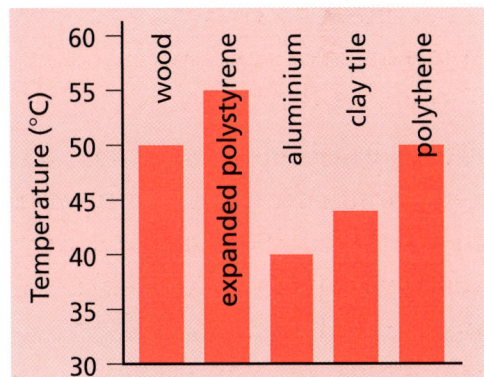

National Curriculum links

■ Experimental and investigative work
■ Analysing evidence and drawing conclusions

To be working at levels 5–8 you need to make predictions and draw conclusions based on scientific knowledge. Your conclusions should take account of the number of results you have collected and be linked to them.

Links with the Classbook

Unit 24 *pages 50–51*
Unit 104 *pages 218–219*
Unit 114 *pages 238–239*

Question:

■ What effect will adding fertiliser have on how tall seedlings grow?

Prediction:

■ The more fertiliser you add, the taller the seedlings will grow. This is because plants need a range of essential elements for growth, which they obtain from the soil. Fertiliser adds these elements to the soil.

Results:

Amount of fertiliser (g/l)	Average height of seedling (cm)
1	5.1
2	6.0
3	7.0
4	7.5
5	8.0
6	8.0
7	8.0

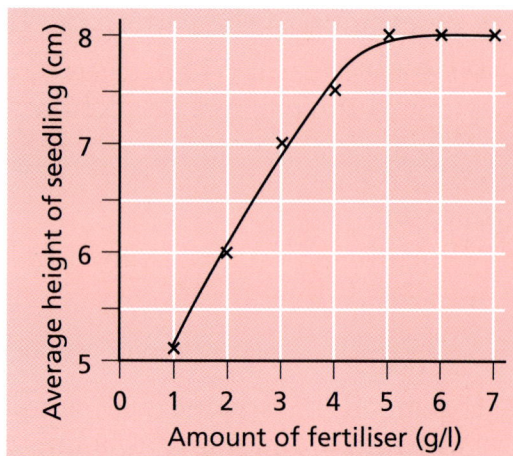

Conclusion:

....

....

....

....

....

National Curriculum links

■ Experimental and investigative work

■ Analysing evidence and drawing conclusions

To be working at levels 5–8 you need to make predictions and draw conclusions based on scientific knowledge. Your conclusions should take account of the number of results you have collected and be linked to them.

Links with the Classbook

Unit 24
pages 50–51

Unit 104
pages 218–219

Unit 114
pages 238–239

There are two types of data, **qualitative** and **quantitative**.

In *Bar charts* (Unit 17) you saw that Karen and Yusif changed the **type** of candle. They made no measurements of the candles themselves. They only measured how long each candle took to go out. They had to draw a bar chart for their results because their data was **qualitative**.

They could have measured the **height** or **thickness** of each candle. If they had done this they would have collected **quantitative** data. They would have measured a quantity. They could then have plotted a line graph of the results.

1 Below are results that could be taken from different investigations. Beside each one write down whether the data is qualitative or quantitative.

Time to react

Extension of a spring

Pulse rate

Time to dissolve

Type of washing powder

Species of plant

Number of bubbles of oxygen

Species of bird

Height of a ramp

2 Write down two more examples of qualitative data.

3 Write down two more examples of quantitative data.

National Curriculum links

- Experimental and investigative work
- Analysing evidence and drawing conclusions

To be working at levels 3–8 you need to be able to present qualitative and quantitative data clearly.

Considering the strength of the data

This diagram shows the important ideas you will cover in this section.

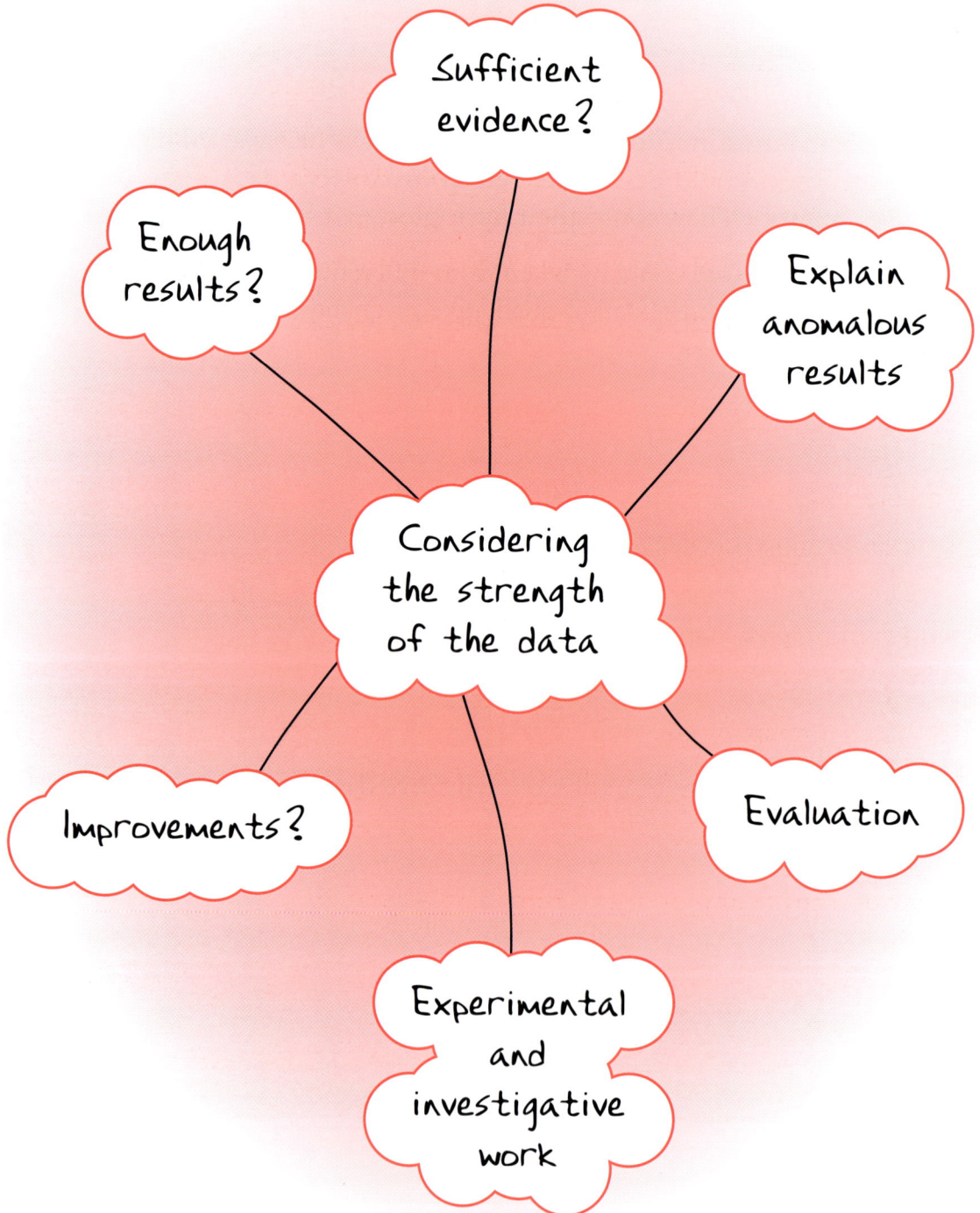

Sufficient evidence?

Enough results?

Explain anomalous results

Considering the strength of the data

Improvements?

Evaluation

Experimental and investigative work

Improving my ability to consider the strength of data

When you work through this part of the book you will pick up tips or advice on how to improve your investigation. This is called **evaluation**. If you have carried out a good investigation, you will have collected very reliable results. When you pick up tips which help you to **consider the reliabilty or strength of your data,** write them down in the spaces below.

There are **three** main areas to consider when evaluating an investigation:

1 How do I know whether I can draw the conclusion I have made from the results I have collected?

....

....

....

2 How do I explain anomalous results?

....

....

....

3 How do I make improvements to my investigation?

....

....

....

When you have carried out and written up an investigation, it is important to look back over the work. This will help you to decide whether the investigation you planned answered your original question as fully as possible. This is called evaluating your work.

Example

Pauline and Inta were investigating the question:

■ Does increasing the concentration of a fertiliser make cress seedlings grow taller?

They set up eight dishes with cotton wool in the bottom and put five cress seeds in each dish. They made eight samples of fertiliser by adding 100 cm^3 of water to eight beakers. They then added 1 spatula of fertiliser powder to the first beaker, 2 spatulas to the second beaker and so on up to 8 spatulas for the eighth beaker. The dishes with seeds were topped up with a few millilitres of fertiliser solution from the beakers over the next few days to keep them moist. After a week they measured the two tallest seedlings in each dish and worked out an average height.

The table of results and graph are shown below:

Amount of fertiliser	Average Height of seedlings
(spatulas)	(mm)
1	2.4
2	7.4
3	8.8
4	10.4
5	9.0
6	11.0
7	11.0
8	10.9

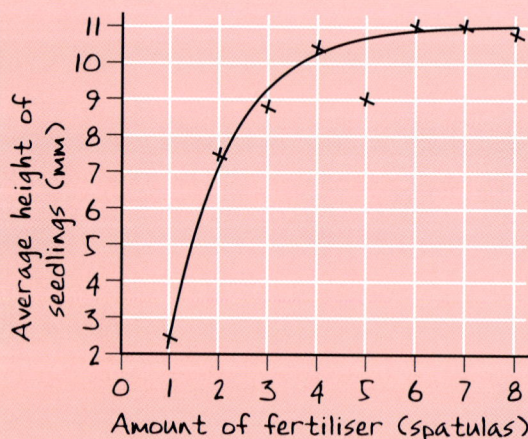

National Curriculum links
- Experimental and investigative work
- Considering the strength of the data

To be working at levels 5–8 you need to be able to draw conclusions that are consistent with your evidence.

Links with the Classbook

Unit 24
pages 50–51

Unit 61
pages 128–129

1 Could Pauline and Inta say in their conclusion that:
'All fertilisers make cress seedlings grow taller?'

....

....

....

....

2 There is an anomalous result at 5 spatulas of fertiliser.
Why do you think this happened and how could it have
been prevented?

....

....

....

....

3 Are there any other suggestions you could make to
improve this investigation?

....

....

....

....

National Curriculum links
- Experimental and investigative work
- Considering the strength of the data

*To be working at levels 5–8 you need to be able to draw
conclusions that are consistent with your evidence.*

Links with the Classbook

Unit 24
pages 50–51

Unit 61
pages 128–129

Now it's your turn

Paul and Max were investigating the question:

■ Do birds prefer peanuts or sunflower seeds for food?

They put both foods in feeders and hung them in different parts of the school grounds. They observed the birds that visited each feeder for about half an hour one morning. The results they collected are shown in the bar charts below.

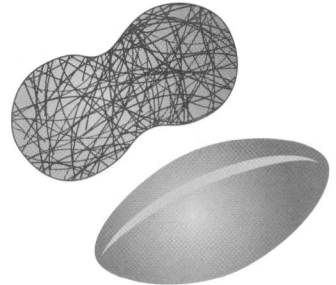

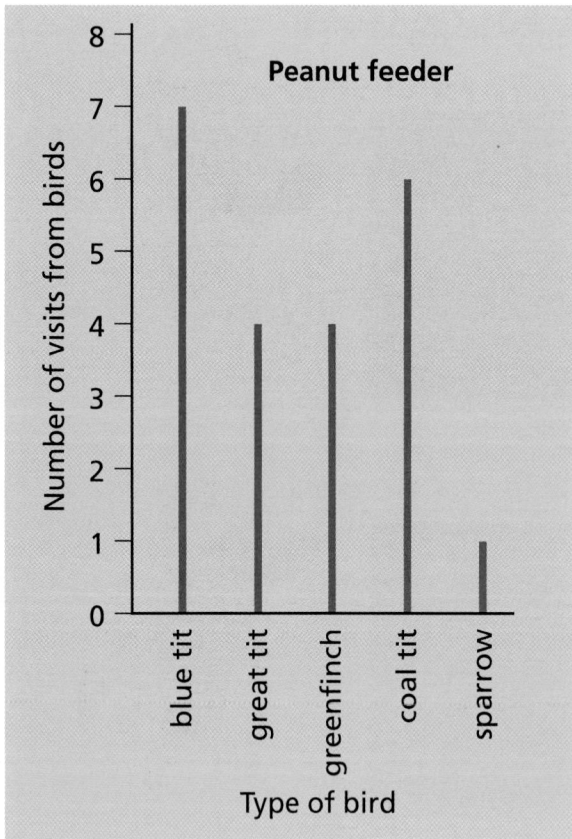

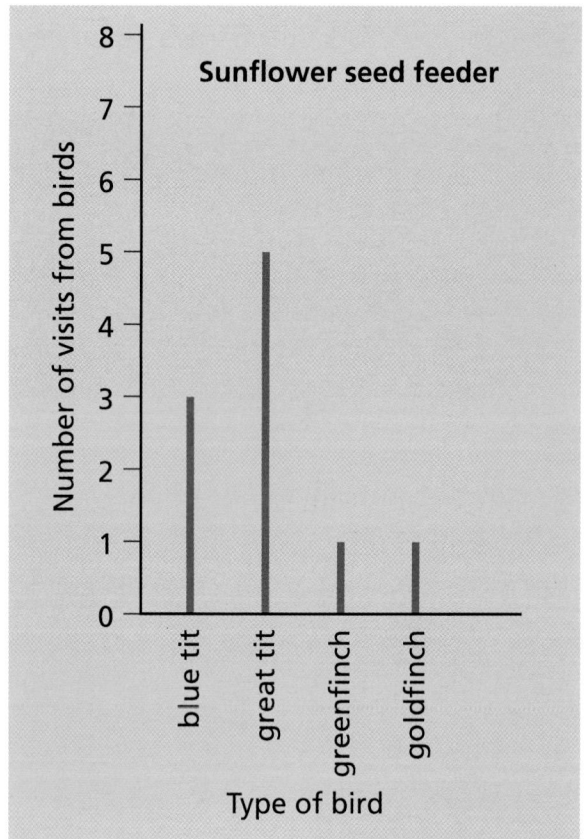

Peanut feeder — Number of visits from birds / Type of bird: blue tit 7, great tit 4, greenfinch 4, coal tit 6, sparrow 1.

Sunflower seed feeder — Number of visits from birds / Type of bird: blue tit 3, great tit 5, greenfinch 1, goldfinch 1.

National Curriculum links

■ Experimental and investigative work

■ Considering the strength of the data

To be working at levels 5–8 you need to be able to draw conclusions that are consistent with your evidence.

Links with the Classbook

Unit 5
pages 12–13

Unit 34
pages 70–71

Paul and Max concluded that:

■ Birds prefer peanuts to sunflower seeds.

1 Can Paul and Max say confidently that all birds prefer peanuts to sunflower seeds for food?

....

....

....

....

2 Can you reword their original question to make it better?

....

....

....

....

3 What improvements would you suggest to the way they did the investigation?

....

....

....

....

National Curriculum links

■ Experimental and investigative work
■ Considering the strength of the data

To be working at levels 5–8 you need to be able to draw conclusions that arc consistent with your evidence.

Links with the Classbook

Unit 5
pages 12–13

Unit 34
pages 70–71

Investigation grid

		1 Planning experimental procedures	2 Obtaining evidence	3 Analysing evidence and drawing conclusions	4 Considering the strength of the data
NATIONAL CIRRICULUM LEVEL	**3**	I can ask a question. I can make a simple prediction.	I can observe things and use simple equipment to make simple measurements. I need some help to carry out a fair test.	I can record my observations. I can see patterns in my results. I can say what I have found out.	
	4	I can ask a question. I can make a simple prediction.	I can carry out a fair test. I can select the correct equipment and make observations and measurements.	I record my results in tables and charts. I can plot simple graphs and recognise patterns or trends in my results. I can say what I have found out and use some science to explain my conclusion.	
	5	I can ask a question. I can make a prediction which has a scientific explanation.	I can carry out a range of tests to answer my question. I use equipment with care and accuracy. I can repeat a test if I get an odd result.	I can record my results systematically in tables. I can plot accurate line graphs. I can say what I have found out and use some science to explain my conclusion.	I can spot anomalous results.
	6	I can ask a question. I can make a prediction which has a scientific explanation.	I can carry out a range of tests to answer my question. I use equipment with complicated scales and make accurate measurements. I can make enough measurements to answer my question.	I can record my results systematically in tables. I can plot accurate line graphs and adjust the scales to best show the results. I can say what I have found out and use science to explain my conclusion.	I can spot anomalous results. I can comment on whether I have collected enough data.
	7	I can ask a question. I can make a prediction which has a scientific explanation.	I can carry out a range of tests to answer my question. I use equipment with complicated scales and make accurate measurements. I can make enough measurements to answer my question.	I can record my results systematically in tables. I can plot accurate line graphs and adjust the scales to best show the results. I can say what I have found out and use science to explain my conclusion.	I can spot anomalous results. I can say whether the data I have collected allows me to make my conclusions.
	8	I can ask a question. I can make a prediction which has a scientific explanation. I can choose the appropriate strategy for obtaining data.	I can carry out a range of tests to answer my question. I use equipment with complicated scales and make accurate measurements. I can make enough measurements to answer my question. I can decide on what level of precision I need to use when measuring.	I can record my results systematically in tables. I can plot accurate line graphs with lines of best fit and adjust the scales to best show the results. I can say what I have found out and use science to explain the shapes of my graphs and my conclusions. I can ignore results which are not relevant or are anomalous.	I can spot anomalous results. I can say whether the data I have collected allows me to make my conclusions. I can identify short-comings in my data.
	Exeptional performance	I can use research to find information in order to ask a question. I can make a quantitative prediction which has a scientific explanation.	I can carry out a range of tests to answer my question. I use equipment with complicated scales and make accurate measurements. I can make enough measurements to answer my question. I can decide on what level of precision I need to use when measuring. I can use my data to test relationships between variables.	I can record my results systematically in tables. I can plot accurate line graphs with lines of best fit and adjust the scales to best show the results. I can say what I have found out and use science to explain the shapes of my graphs and my conclusions. I can ignore results which are not relevant or are anomalous.	I can spot anomalous results. I can say whether the data I have collected allows me to make my conclusions. I can identify what further data I need to collect to allow me to make improvements to my investigation.

Now you have covered this section fill in the missing words.

Planning
experimental
work

Now you have covered this section fill in the missing words.

Obtaining
evidence

Now you have covered this section fill in the missing words.

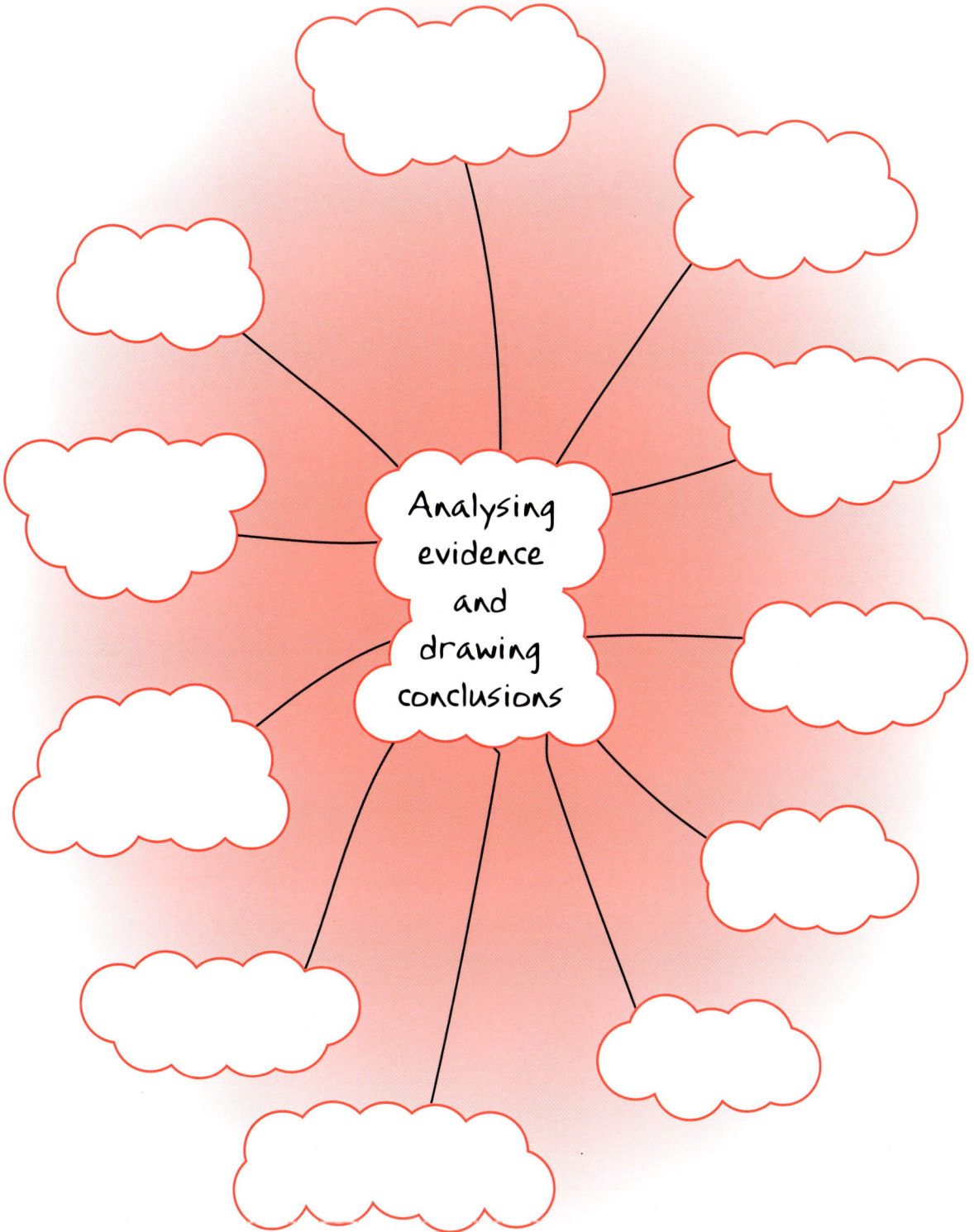

Analysing evidence and drawing conclusions

Now you have covered this section fill in the missing words.

Considering the strength of the data